17-76 Tea Party
Award-Winning Recipes

17 Jams and Butters
76 Scones and Biscuits

Tastes of Home,
Colours of the Past

Jennifer C. Petersen
Cuppa Countess

A Cuppa Countess Gourmet Guide

17-76 Tea Party Recipes

Tastes of Home, Colours of the Past

A Cuppa Countess Gourmet Guide

By
Jennifer C. Petersen

© Copyright 2010
By
Tea Trade Mart Publishing Co.
800 NE Tenney Road, 110-107
Vancouver, WA 98685
www.TeaTradeMart.com

Printed and manufactured in
The United States of America.
ISBN-978-0-9705003-3-5

ISBN: 978-0-9705003-3-5

51995

9 780970 500335

Publication #13,471
G & R Publishing Company
800-383-1679
www.gandrpublishing.com

Table of Contents

CHAPTER 3   CUPPA COUNTESS GOURMET GUIDE & REFERENCES

Foreword by J.N. Pratt

JAMES NORWOOD PRATT

Jennifer Petersen is dear to me and has been these many years since tea first brought us together. In a quiet sort of way we have shared a good many tea adventures over the years since.

Sharing is what Jennifer's all about---I told you she's a dear---and now she's sharing all that lore and learning how to make things scrumptious with just anybody lucky enough to open her book. I advise you take tea with Jennifer and let her share, in her quiet sort of way, the sort of teatime pleasures that make her and me smile when we're together.

Can tea have political implications, do you suppose? How, back in North Carolina back in 1776, would our ancestors have greeted Jennifer's "Buckingham Palace Scones", I wonder? In that era this recipe would separate the patriots from the Tory loyalists of the day, just as the term "tea party" again involves deeply felt politics in our time.

Tea itself, however, is a sure cure for upsets of every sort and will hush our rancors with peace and pleasure if we let it. That's what my dear Jennifer will tell you: Make tea, not trouble.

Peace,
James Norwood Pratt

Born in Winston-Salem, North Carolina, and brought up on land which has been in his family since before the American Revolution, **James Norwood Pratt** was educated at Chapel Hill and abroad and published his first book on tea in 1982.

Whether as Honorary Director of America's first traditional Chinese teahouse or as International Juror of India's first-ever tea competition, James Norwood Pratt has served the cause of tea around the world for thirty years as author, instigator, and teacher. He is America's acknowledged Tea Sage and quite possibly the world's most widely read authority on tea and tea lore.

Judith Krall-Russo is a New Jersey native. As an independent scholar and lecturer, Judith has research food history, especially the foods and customs of her home state, New Jersey.

Ms. Krall-Russo received certification from The Tea School in Pomfret, Connecticut, in 2000. She is certified Level 4 by The Specialty Tea Institute in New York City and is a long time student of the Japanese Tea Ceremony at the Urasenke Chanoyu Center also in New York City. Judith holds an MBA from Pace University (NY) and a BA from Montclair State University (NJ). Judith is a sought after speaker and consultant, and is known for her enthusiastic, inspiring style and knowledgeable presentations. She is the owner of www.teafoodhistory.com.

Pat Stephens – Assistant Special Sections Editor, The Columbian, Advertising Department, Vancouver, WA

For the past several years, Pat Stephens served as assistant special sections editor for The Columbian Newspaper's advertising division, in Vancouver, Washington, and met Jennifer through her work. Pat enjoys reading, needlework and sewing, and volunteers for several community organizations.

Pat Jollota – Past Curator, Clark County Historical Museum (18 years)

Pat Jollota's curriculum vitae reads like an international Who's Who in community service. Born in Los Angeles, California, Ms. Jollota served for 22 years with the LAPD. In Great Britain, she was the general manager at the Queen's Hotel, Newbury, Berks, and U.K. Coincidentally, she was Curator of Education at the Clark County Historical Museum and served as a Vancouver City Councilmember for 20 years. Her past board affiliations and commissions would fill its own book.

As founder of the non-profit group, Justice for Children, Pat Jollota devotes time and talent as a member of the Clark County Historical Promotion Committee and is a member of the boards of directors for eight charitable organizations including the ARC of Clark County.

Pat writes: "Vancouver Washington has been blessed with a vibrant personality named Jennifer Petersen. I've never known her to be anything but upbeat in everything that she does. This is reflected in this delightful collection of recipes.

There was once a charming little shop in our city called Carnelian Rose Tea. One could browse for an unexpected treat, or seriously discuss teas, coffees, sugars and creams. It was a place for those who searched for the real thing, real tea, real sugar, and real food. There is a flavor of that shop in this book because Jennifer was the hostess of that establishment. How lucky for us all that she has given us this glimpse into the wonderful goodies we've shared."

EE Harris – University of Kansas, Lawrence, Kansas
"*Tastes of Home, Colours of the Past* is very readable and informative – makes you want to peek inside, then make a bee-line for the kitchen!"

JENNIFER BYERS PETERSEN

Jennifer Petersen lives alongside a creek in a quiet old-growth forest in the State of Washington. A "Southern Lady" by heritage, born in the Western North Carolina area of the Blue Ridge Mountains, Jennifer Petersen baked her first cake at the age of eight and baked her first buttermilk biscuits soon afterwards. Her interest in genealogy grew as a result of tracing her Irish and English ancestors who arrived in Virginia around 1528. The Cuppa Countess' lineage includes ancestors from many different countries and she is Cherokee Proud.

The owner of Carnelian Rose Tea Co, she owned a tea and gift shop for over twelve years. The 17-76 scone and jam recipes are from the *Chandelier Room* master cookbook that received rave reviews from tea customers and tea students alike.

Jennifer Petersen is a tea business development consultant and a masterful tea blender to the trade. She helps tea professionals start a tea business and she develops tea-training programs for food and beverage companies.

The director of Tea Business School, Ms. Petersen is a professional trainer who conducts tea training seminars. A graduate of the Protocol School of Washington®, Petersen's programs include business etiquette and protocol. The "Cuppa Countess", is a member of the Specialty Tea Institute, STI Tea Advisory Board past, DAR Fort Vancouver Chapter, Clark County Genealogical Society, and Women Entrepreneur's Organization.

In respectful memory of my mother and grandmothers,

Betty Sue McClure Granstrom

Jennie Mae Coleman McClure

Gurlie Ashe Byers

Eliza Canzadie Ledford Byers

Sarah Isabella Farmer Coleman

Jane Elizabeth Kilpatrick Coleman

Lucy White Coleman

Sarah Isabella Countryman Bryson

For my blue-ribbon sister, Vicki Lynn Byers Cartwright
who does, indeed, make the best biscuits in our family.
And for my sister, Charlotte Diane Byers Oden,
who is best at setting the table.

From tea rooms to home patio, simple to elegant,
chandeliers to lamplight, when you share time-honored
tea traditions and scrumptious recipes with family and friends –
you'll create your own…..

Tastes of Home – Colours of the Past

Family Tree

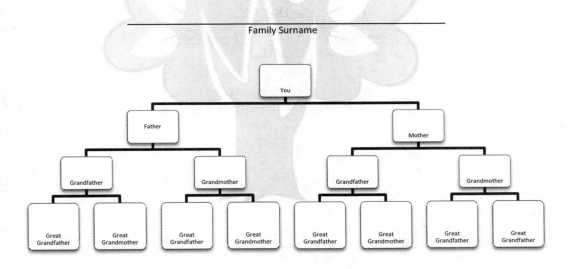

Family Surname

When you have gathered all the information you need,
write your family members' names – generation by generation.
It makes a perfect visual reminder of your heritage
or a family history gift for other family members.

Favorite Photographs

Family
Photographs
or
Memorable
Tea Parties

Cuppa Countess Guide for Tea

How to Make a Perfect Cup of Tea

For hot tea

Preheat a teapot by rinsing it out with hot water. Bring fresh, non-chlorinated cold water to a full rolling boil. Water that has been reheated gives tea a flat taste; only boiling water can extract the full flavor and benefit from black tea leaves. A good way to judge the temperature of water is this: when watching a pot of water cup to a boil, the first bubbles that appear in the bottom are "fish eyes". When the bubbles begin to rise to the surface, they are sometimes called a "strand of pearls". Lastly, when air bubbles cover the water surface and it rolls, it is a "full boil".

Steep white and green teas at 170°-185°F or at the "fish eye" stage. Steep oolong at 185°F to 200°F or at the "strand of pearls" stage. Black tea is steeped at 200°F to 212°F. Green and white teas will recoil if boiling water is used - making a bitter flavor. Some teas may be infused multiple times creating a different sensory pleasure with each infusion.

Use one teaspoonful of tea or one teabag per cup of water and pour the hot water over the tea. (The precise measure is typically 2g tea to 5 oz. water.) Steep for 3 to 7 minutes. Don't judge the strength of tea by its color and allow time for the leaves to unfold and release their flavor. If you like tea less strong, add water after the brewing period. If tea is too weak however, you must begin again.

For iced tea

Follow the guidelines for making hot tea, but use 50% more tea to allow for melting ice. For a pitcher of iced tea, bring 1 quart of fresh water to a full rolling boil. Remove from heat and immediately add one-third cup of loose tea. Stir and let stand 5 minutes. Stir again and strain into a pitcher holding an additional quart of fresh cold water.

Do You Know About Tea?

Loose-leaf tea (*camellia sinensis*) has different processing methods that determine whether or not it is a white tea, green tea, oolong tea, black tea or pu-erh? Tea descriptions are also determined by terroir and grading classifications.

Over sixty countries produce tea including the United States of America and Great Britain. First grown in China, tea as a beverage was an accidental discovery when, as the traditional story goes, a tea leaf floated by happenstance into a pot of boiling water about 2500 years ago. The resulting beverage was discovered to be tasty and to provide a mild lift to energy – components we now recognize as mild caffeine and other health benefits.

Teabag vs. loose-leaf: in addition to loose-leaf teas' greater health benefits, loose-leaf tea provides a broader wealth of selection which means there is more than likely a tea to suit anyone's palate. Tea leaves like to give each tea sipper their best effort and therefore do better after the uninhibited, serendipitous twirl in a teapot rather than constrained in a teabag.

Recognized a financial trading commodity since the years of the Silk Road, tea remains a hot commodity in today's financial markets and at global tea auctions. Tea is an earth-friendly plant whose producers recognize biodynamic agriculture, organic certification and fair trade regulations.

Today, tea is the global beverage of choice second only to water as the number one beverage drank 'round the world.

Guide for a Bountiful Tea Tray

The elements of a bountiful tea tray are basically the same whether you are using a three tiered silver buffet type server or designing single-serve tea plates.

The perfect tea party is all about creating a sensual tea experience for one's guests. Questions to guide you:

- **What will they see?** Are the jams colourful and the scones baked in various shapes? Are the tea trays enhanced with flowers or ribbons or antique servers? Is there elevation and depth to the placement rather than everything flat?

- **What will they smell?** Are the scones fresh out of the oven?

- **What will they hear?** Will ambient background sound be light music or outdoor garden party sounds of birds and crickets or perhaps silence?

- **What will they touch?** Is all food "finger food" or will guests need serving tongs along with a fork, knife and spoon? Are teacups easy to handle for everyone?

- **What will they taste?** Is the tea prepared properly without leaving the tea leaves or teabags in the pot? Are savory scones paired with an herbal butter spread, clotted cream or plain butter?

Guide for Tea Food Placement

Dining etiquette suggests that tea food be served and eaten from the bottom tier upwards although antique tiered tea servers were equipped with a scone warmer on the top tier. The effect is the same: the top tier is left intact for visual appeal throughout tea time.

1. Bottom tier: sandwiches and savories

2. Middle tier: scones

3. Top tier: desserts and sweets

4. Fruit and flowers add bright, appetizing spots to any tea plate or tea tier.

Desserts and Sweets

Scones and Tea Breads

Tea Sandwiches and Savories

Unusual tea servers add a different dimension to beautiful tea service. Patterned bone china plates, cream ware, clear glass, mirrors, wicker, bamboo and pottery are appropriate for various occasions aside from a traditional silver tea tray. My favorite tea tray is an old wicker tray, 8"x10", with red and blue wooden beads. Lined with a tea towel and heaped with scones and jam – it's low-key but stunning.

Will you go into the Tea Time Hall of Shame if you do otherwise? Of course not!

Herb and Spice Substitutions

If you grow an herb garden or have access to a fresh farmer's market, you'll find the taste of some herbs and spices are somewhat similar. You can substitute measure for measure the following herbs and spices:

Herbs and Fruits

Basil and Oregano
Caraway and Anise
Celery Seeds and Minced Celery Tops
Chervil and Parsley
Chervil and Tarragon
Fennel and Anise
Fennel and Tarragon
Oregano and Marjoram
Lemon and Lime
Blackberry, Marionberry and Raspberries

Spices

Masala chai and equal parts Cinnamon, Cardamom, and Pepper
Nutmeg and Mace
Mace and Cardamom

Cuppa Countess Cooking Tips

Note: Some of the recipes in 17-76 Tastes of Home, Colours of the Past may have similar ingredients, but the results are markedly different. For example, there are four blueberry scone recipes and each is very different. Recipes were created for your enjoyment and are not meant to be historically significant.

Sugar Free Recipes: Baked goods made without sugar do not brown well and will need checked to determine when they are finished baking. Purchase the sweetener substitutes **clearly labeled for baking or cooking.**

In general, here are sweetener substitutions:
· Stevia (1 tsp. ground stevia equals one cup sugar)
· Sweet N Low™ (2 tsp. equals 1/2 cup sugar)
· Sweet N Low™ liquid (4 tsp. equals 1/2 cup sugar)
· Sweet One™ (6 packets equals 1/2 cup sugar)

A few drops of lemon juice added to whipping cream helps it whip faster and better.

Cream whipped ahead of time will not separate if you add 1/4 teaspoon unflavored gelatin per cup of cream.

Finely dicing a cold stick of butter saves pastry blending time.

Before measuring honey or other syrup, oil the cup with cooking oil and rinse in hot water.

Try adding a teaspoonful of candied or preserved ginger to your apple recipes this year.

Tiny tea biscuits make an excellent foundation for sweet sandwiches. They are split and buttered while hot and filled with honey and almonds, cream cheese and jam, or chopped nuts and marmalade.

Cut rolled scone dough with a biscuit cutter, going straight down and straight up. If you twist, scones will be lopsided when baked.

To remove mineral deposits from tea kettles, fill with equal parts vinegar and water. Bring to a boil and allow standing overnight.

To remove tea stains from fine china, rub with a damp cloth dipped in baking soda.

Do's and Taboos of Scones

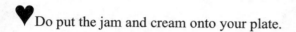 Do put the jam and cream onto your plate.

Taboo: taking jam directly from the jam jar and placing it directly on the scone.

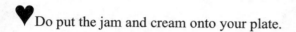 Do take only the amount of butter, jam, marmalade or cream needed.

Taboo: putting more spread on your plate than needed for one scone.

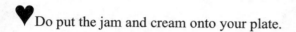 Do rest your used butter knife on the plate.

Taboo: soiling the table linen by returning the used knife to the table.

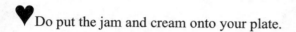 Do put jam and then cream on your scone in this order.

Taboo: slathering the scone with cream and then balancing a large blog of jam on the top.

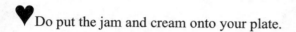 Do break off bite size pieces of scone, spread with butter or jam and cream then convey to the mouth.

Taboo with a capital "T": slicing a scone, filling it with jam and cream, and consuming it like a fast food sandwich.

Butters, Jams, Marmalades and Jellies

Butter:

butter (ˈbʌtə)

— *n*

2. any substance with a butter-like consistency, such as apple butter, peanut butter or vegetable butter

[Old English *butere,* from Latin *būtyrum,* from Greek *bouturon,* from *bous* cow + *turos* cheese]

Jam:

jam [2] (dʒæm)

— *n*

1. a preserve containing fruit, which has been boiled with sugar until the mixture sets

[C18: perhaps from jam [1] (the act of squeezing)]

Jelly:

jelly [1] (ˈdʒɛlɪ)

— *n, pl* **-lies**

2. a preserve made from the juice of fruit boiled with sugar and used as jam

[C14: from Old French *gelee* frost, jelly, from *geler* to set hard, from Latin *gelāre,* from *gelu* frost]

Marmalade:

marmalade (ˈmɑːməˌleɪd)

— *n*

1. A preserve made by boiling the pulp and rind of citrus fruits, esp. oranges, with sugar

[C16: via French from Portuguese *marmelada,* from *marmelo* quince, from Latin, from Greek *melimēlon,* from *meli* honey + *mēlon* apple

History and Tradition of Scones

/Scone\, n. A cake, thinner than a bannock, made of wheat or barley or oat meal. [Written variously, scon, skone, skon, etc.] [Scot.] --Burns.

The origin of the word scone is debatable. Some say it comes from the Dutch word schoonbrot (beautiful bread) and others say that the name comes from the Stone of Destiny (or Scone). This pastry takes its name from a Scottish village near Perth. The village of Scone was the site of the Stone of Destiny, a large stone brought to the kingdom in the eighth century upon which Scottish kings were once crowned. Scottish kings were upon this stone for more than a thousand years. The present British Queen Elizabeth II was crowned on the Stone in 1953.

The original triangular-shaped scone was made with oats and griddle-baked. Today's versions are more often flour-based and baked in the oven. They come in various shapes including triangles, rounds, squares, and diamonds. They were originally Scottish quick breads with a texture half way between cake and biscuits (harder than a cake but softer than a biscuit). Golden brown in color with a soft inside, they were cut in half and served warm with butter and jam or lemon curd.

The Romans and the Greeks perhaps created the ancestor to the scone: a somewhat dense cake sweetened with honey. These cakes were often grain-based or made with nuts or cheese. The resulting varieties then spread to the British Isles as Roman expansion continued throughout Europe. Scottish bannocks (made from barley) were thick, hearty little cakes that were prepared on a griddle over the fire. The cake was sliced into quarters and turned over to cook the other side. The wedges were called scones. With the advent of baking powder, scones became lighter and more palatable. Like the biscuit, there are many varieties of scones. The Irish and Scots began to migrate west to the Americas, and the scone followed.

The scone derives from the Scottish Bannock which was a soft cake of barley meal baked on an iron plate known as a girdle (Scots language for griddle), the forerunner to the hotplate. The Bannock was round and cut into four pieces, making it easier to turn over during baking. When cut, the individual triangle of Bannock was now a scone. With the introduction of baking soda, buttermilk, and wheat flours, a softer and lighter scone evolved. As shown in this scone recipe collection, today we have an array of scone variants; butter, whole meal, herb, cheese, fruited, chocolate chip, drop, honey, potato and many more.

Returning to baking methods, scones were originally prepared on a griddle over a stove. As baking ovens became more popular, people probably tried baking the scones in an oven. Due to their wedge-like shape, it was difficult to cook them evenly in the early, temperamental stoves. The edges would burn and become dry. By cutting the dough into rounds the scones cooked more evenly. Some people think that the Dutch learned the basic ingredient proportions of the scone from the Scotch/Irish and they treated the dough as they would their "koekje" (cake). After rolling out the dough, they probably cut it into round shapes with their cutters thereby creating the biscuit. In the mélange of language and culture, the English term 'biscuit' was probably mistakenly applied to the scone.

The scone/biscuit recipes crossed the Atlantic with Early American immigrants and met yet another mix of cultures and availability of ingredients in the new country. Once again it probably took another evolution and became the traditional American biscuit.

As my ancestors migrated from Virginia and the Pennsylvania Dutch County, down the Appalachian and McClure wagon trails into Tennessee, North Carolina and Georgia, they must have baked many batches of scones (and hush puppies—but then that's another story). Although they originated so many years and miles away, the scone remains part of our everyday lives and especially of our tea celebrations.

Jams and Spreads

Chai Apple Butter

All Star Lemon Curd

5	whole egg yolks	4	whole lemons, zested and juiced
1	cup sugar	1/2 cup	butter, cold and diced

Procedure

In double boiler, add enough water to bottom saucepan to come about 1-inch up the side. Bring to a simmer over medium-high heat. Meanwhile, combine egg yolks and sugar in upper saucepan and whisk until smooth, about 1 minute. Measure citrus juice and if needed, add enough cold water to reach 1/3 cup. Add juice and zest to egg mixture and whisk smooth. Once water reaches a simmer, reduce heat to low and place small saucepan on top of lower saucepan. Whisk until thickened, approximately 8 minutes, or until mixture is light yellow and coats the back of a spoon. Remove promptly from heat and stir in butter a piece at a time, allowing each addition to melt before adding the next. Remove to a clean container and cover by laying a layer of plastic wrap directly on the surface of the curd to prevent skin. Refrigerate for up to 2 weeks.

Yield: 1 pint

Nutrition Facts

Nutrition (per serving): 81 calories, 42 calories from fat, 4.8g total fat, 52.8mg cholesterol, 2.7mg sodium, 31.2mg potassium, 10.4g carbohydrates, <1g fiber, 8.4g sugar, <1g protein.

Betsy's Blackberry Curd

1 cup sugar
3 Tbs. cornstarch
2 cups blackberry juice

3 large eggs, slightly beaten
2 egg yolks
1/4 cup butter

Procedure

Combine sugar and cornstarch in a 3-quart saucepan; gradually whisk in blackberry juice. Whisk in eggs and egg yolks. Bring mixture to a boil (5 or 6 minutes) over medium heat, whisking constantly.

Cook, whisking constantly, 1 to 2 minutes or until a pudding-like thickness. Remove from heat and whisk in butter. Cover, placing plastic wrap directly on curd. Chill for 8 hours.

Note: After chilling, fillings and sauces thickened with cornstarch will loosen when stirred. Don't stir after chilling! Just spoon the curd directly into tart shells or spoon and spread over cake layers.

Yield: 3 cups blackberry curd

Nutrition Facts

Nutrition (per serving): 35 calories, 3 calories from fat, 1.48g total fat, 24.5mg cholesterol, 5mg sodium, 11mg potassium, 5g carbohydrates, <1g fiber, 4.51g sugar, <1g protein.

Blackberry, Lavender and Sage Jelly

1 3/4 cups blackberry juice (see "Bonus Recipe 2")

1	cup	lavender water
1	cup	sage water
1	box	fruit pectin
1/2	tsp.	butter or margarine
4 1/2		cups sugar

Lavender Water

1	cup	water
1/4	cup	lavender flowers

Sage Water

1	cup	water
1/4	cup	sage leaves

Procedure

LAVENDER WATER

Bring one cup water and 1/4 cup chopped lavender petals to boil. Steep for one hour. Strain before using.

SAGE WATER

Bring one cup of water and 1/4 cup finely chopped fresh sage leaves to boil. Steep for 1 hour. Strain before using.

JELLY

Make jelly: measure exactly 1-3/4 cups juice, one cup lavender water, and 1 cup sage water into 6- or 8-qt. saucepot. Stir pectin into juice in saucepot. Add butter to reduce foaming. Bring mixture to full rolling boil on high heat, stirring constantly. Stir in sugar. Return to full rolling boil and boil one minute stirring constantly. Remove from heat and ladle into jars; seal. Process jars in hot water bath, or cool then keep refrigerated.

Yield: Six half-pints of jelly

Nutrition Facts

Nutrition (per serving): 55 calories, <1 calories from fat, <1g total fat, <1mg cholesterol, 1.2mg sodium, 3.7mg potassium, 14.2g carbohydrates, <1g fiber, 13.7g sugar, <1g protein.

Carnelian Rose Petal Jam

30	large red organic cabbage roses	2	quarts water
6	cups granulated sugar	1	Tbs. lemon juice

Procedure

Cut the white ends and hips off the roses. In a large pot, make a syrup with the sugar and water. Then add the juice of half a lemon and the rose petals. Boil until the roses crystallize and become transparent, stirring frequently with a wooden spoon. Reduce by 1/2 or until jam like consistency. Pour into sterilized containers and seal per jar manufacturer's instructions.

No damask cabbage roses? Simply substitute 4 tablespoons rose water for part of the liquid.

Yield: 4 pints

Nutrition Facts

Nutrition (per serving): 35 calories, 0 calories from fat, 0g total fat, 0mg cholesterol, <1mg sodium, <1mg potassium, 9.1g carbohydrates, 0g fiber, 9.1g sugar, 0g protein.

Cuppa Countess Comment: After the British capture of Charleston, South Carolina, The Battle of Kings Mountain on October 7, 1780 was a pivotal day in the War of Independence. Herbert Hoover said: "...inspired by the urge of freedom....It was a little army and a little battle, but it was of mighty portent."

One of my grandmothers, Sarah Isabella Countryman Bryson, carried water to the troops at the Battle of King's Mountain. Born in Pennsylvania in 1750, she married James Holmes Bryson in 1769 in King's Mountain, South Carolina.

Chai Apple Butter

12 lbs. Granny Smith apples - peeled, cored and sliced	1/4 tsp. ground cloves
1/2 cup golden balsamic vinegar	1 tsp. ground cardamom
3 cups white sugar	1/2 tsp. ground ginger
1 cup brown sugar	1/2 tsp. ground white pepper
1 Tbs. ground cinnamon	

Procedure

Make in a crock-pot and no stirring, no sticking ~ just lots of great aroma and flavor!

Place apples and vinegar into a large crock-pot and place lid on top. Set on High, and cook for 8 hours, then turn to Low, and cook for 10 more hours.

After 18 hours, stir in white sugar, brown sugar, and spices then cook 4 hours more. Ladle into hot, sterilized half-pint jars. Process in hot water bath for 20 minutes.

Yield: 12 half-pints

Nutrition Facts

Nutrition (per serving): 121 calories, 1 calories from fat, <1g total fat, 0mg cholesterol, 1.9mg sodium, 122.1mg potassium, 31.7g carbohydrates, 1.6g fiber, 28.4g sugar, <1g protein.

Cranberry Honey Spread

2 cups unsalted butter, room temperature

1/2 cup cranberries, coarsely chopped

1/4 cup light brown sugar

1/4 cup honey

4 Tbs. ground walnuts

1/2 cup whole cranberry sauce

1 Tbs. grated orange zest

1 tsp. grated lemon zest

2 Tbs. buttermilk

Procedure

In a large bowl, whip the softened butter at high speed with an electric mixer until it turns pale yellow, scraping the sides of the bowl to make sure all the butter is whipped.

Add the cranberries, sugar, honey, walnuts, cranberry sauce and orange zest and lemon zest. Whip at medium speed until the mixture turns light pink. Add the buttermilk and whip until fully incorporated.

Cranberry Butter can be covered and stored in the mixing bowl or transferred to smaller bowls for storage. Optional: refrigerate for 5 minutes to firm up slightly and then shape into a log approximately 1 inch in diameter for easy slicing into circles.

Wrap securely and store in the refrigerator for 1 to 2 weeks or freeze for up to 3 months.

Yield: 3 cups

Nutrition Facts

Nutrition (per serving): 32 calories, 4 calories from fat, <1g total fat, <1mg cholesterol, 1.8mg sodium, 10.1mg potassium, 7.1g carbohydrates, <1g fiber, 3g sugar, <1g protein.

Crème Chantilly

2	cups heavy cream	1	tsp.	vanilla extract
2	Tbs. granulated sugar			

Procedure

In a large mixing bowl, beat the heavy cream, sugar, and vanilla extract together on high speed until soft peaks form in the mixture. Chill any unused Crème Chantilly. Makes one pint (or enough cream for one average-size cake or pastry recipe).

Yield: 1 pint

Nutrition Facts

Nutrition (per serving): 58 calories, 49 calories from fat, 5.5g total fat, 20.5mg cholesterol, 5.7mg sodium, 11.6mg potassium, 2g carbohydrates, 0g fiber, 1.6g sugar, <1g protein.

Crème Chantilly - Rich whipped cream infused with vanilla extract is a classic embellishment to scones, French pastries, Génoise cakes, and tarts.

Coffee, tea and chocolate were popular non-alcoholic hot beverages during American Colonial times. These imports were expensive, but not beyond the reach of the average person. Folks too poor to afford the *real thing* brewed hot beverages from herbs, flowers, bark, roots, and woody stems. Alas, there was no ready substitute for chocolate! Presumably, cider was served warm too.

"The slave labor system and the expansion of international trade that brought sugar, molasses, and rum into prominence also led to the rise of three new nonalcoholic drinks: chocolate, tea, and coffee." (Fitzgerald, 2004)

Earl Grey Fancy Jelly

3 cups water

12 Earl Grey tea bags

1/2 cup grapefruit juice

1/2 cup orange juice

6 cups sugar

2 3-oz packages liquid pectin

Procedure

Bring water to boil, add tea bags, and steep for 30 minutes. Discard tea bags. Add sugar and juice to steeped tea and bring to a boil.

Boil for 2 minute stirring constantly. Remove from heat and add pectin, return to boil and boil for 1 minute. Remove from heat and skim off any foam. Pour hot jelly into jars and process for 20 minutes in hot water bath.

Yield: Makes 6 half-pints.

Nutrition Facts

Nutrition (per serving): 53 calories, <1 calories from fat, <1g total fat, 0mg cholesterol, 3.2mg sodium, 16mg potassium, 13.8g carbohydrates, <1g fiber, 12.7g sugar, <1g protein.

Cuppa Countess Comment: It is amazing how much children learn by observation. My mother and grandmother took great patience in explaining how to bake and how to create tasty, colourful recipes from few ingredients.
In between explanations, their actions spoke an easy-to-learn language that leant the impression that cooking, family and love are somehow all the same word.

Edible Petal Butter

1	cup	butter, at room temperature	6	Tbs.	confectioners' sugar, sifted
1/2	cup	fresh, edible flowers (petals only), washed and dried	1	tsp.	extract (almond, vanilla, lemon, or orange), optional

Procedure

Place butter, sugar, and extract in food processor, mix until well blended. Add flowers; blend. Makes about 1 1/4 cup.

Serve Flower Power Butter immediately or it is also stunning when chilled in a butter mold for 30 minutes then unmolded onto a serving dish.

Yield: 1 1/4 cup

Nutrition Facts

Nutrition (per serving): 61 calories, 54 calories from fat, 6.2g total fat, 16.3mg cholesterol, <1mg sodium, 5.1mg potassium, 1.7g carbohydrates, <1g fiber, 1.6g sugar, <1g protein.

Try pairing your choice of edible petals with an extract that evokes visual and taste appeal. For example, rose water with red rose petals; grape flavoring with violet petals; peppermint extract with mint leaves; let your imagination be your guide!

Georgia Peach Marmalade

1	each small orange	3	lbs.	fresh peaches
1	each lemon	1	pkg.	dry fruit pectin
1/4 cup	oolong tea, steeped	5	cups sugar	

Procedure

Cut orange and lemon in quarters; remove seeds. Cut the orange and lemon quarters crosswise into very thin slices. In a medium saucepan combine orange and lemon slices and tea. Cover and simmer the orange and lemon mixture over low heat for 20 minutes. Peel, pit, and finely chop peaches. In an 8- to 10- quart kettle, combine orange and lemon mixture and chopped peaches.

Stir pectin into fruit mixture and bring mixture to full rolling boil. Stir in sugar; bring once again to a full rolling boil, stirring constantly. Boil hard, uncovered, 1 minute. Remove from heat; quickly skim off foam. Pour at once into hot sterilized jars; seal.

Yield: 8 half-pints

Nutrition Facts

Nutrition (per serving): 38 calories, <1g from fat, <1g total fat, 0mg cholesterol, .85mg sodium, 24mg potassium, 10g carbohydrates, <1g fiber, 9g sugar, <1g protein.

Which oolong? Green Dragon (Tung Ting or Dong Ding style – meaning "Frozen Summit" or "Ice Peak") works well and Ancient Beauty Jasmine gives a nice twist. Oolong is a production stage in between green tea and black tea. It makes a good hot cup of tea and a splendid iced tea.

Lavender Honey

2 cups honey, clover or flower
1 cup lavender flowers, fresh or 1/2 cup dried lavender flowers

2 sprigs lavender flowers, optional

Procedure

Heat 2 cups of light honey in a double boiler. Add one cup of fresh lavender buds, or 1/2 cup of dried lavender petals. Stir on low heat for 30 minutes. Remove from heat and allow to partially cool. Strain and pour into a sterilized jar.

Yield: One pint

Nutrition Facts

Nutrition (per serving): 43 calories, 0 calories from fat, 0g total fat, 0mg cholesterol, <1mg sodium, 7.4mg potassium, 11.6g carbohydrates, <1g fiber, 11.6g sugar, <1g protein.

"The young ladies of Boston signed a pledge, 'We the daughters of those patriots who have, and do now appear for the public interest, and in that principally regard their posterity, as do with pleasure engage with them in denying ourselves the drinking of foreign tea, in hope to frustrate a plan that tends to deprive a whole community of all that is valuable to life.' Others joined them around the country, drinking instead 'Balsamic Hyperion' made from dried raspberry leaves, or infusions of other herbs. The Boston Tea Party did not destroy the American taste for tea, although few retailers in Boston dared to offer it for sale for a number of years. George and Martha Washington continued to serve the best quality tea." (Pettigrew, 2001)

Minted Pineapple Lime Marmalade

2	whole pineapples (7 cups pineapple, drained)	1/4 cup	fresh mint leaves
		1/2 cup	crème de menthe liqueur
5	whole limes, quartered	1/4 cup	mint leaves, fresh
6	cups sugar		

Procedure

Peel and core the pineapples. Seed the limes, if necessary. Grind the pineapple with the limes in a meat grinder, using the coarsest blade. Put in a large pot with the sugar. Tie the bunch of mint securely, add to the pot and bring the mixture to a boil. Turn heat low, cover the pot and simmer for 1/2 hour, or until the fruits and rind are tender. Uncover, turn up the heat and boil vigorously until the mixture thickens and the juices become syrupy. Remove from heat, discard the bunch of mint, stir in the crème de menthe and the chopped mint leaves and pour into hot, sterilized jelly glasses. Process for 20 minutes in a hot water bath.

Yield: Six half-pints

Nutrition Facts

Nutrition (per serving): 55 calories, <1 calories from fat, <1g total fat, 0mg cholesterol, <1mg sodium, 8.3mg potassium, 13.7g carbohydrates, <1g fiber, 12.9g sugar, <1g protein.

This makes a bittersweet marmalade. To eliminate the bitter lime rind taste, quarter the limes and soak them in cold water to cover for 12 hours prior to making the pineapple-lime marmalade. Drain the limes and proceed as above.

Orange Tipsy Cream

1	8 oz. package reduced-fat cream cheese, softened	1	tsp.	vanilla extract
3	Tbs. sugar	1	tsp.	grated orange peel
1	tsp. orange-flavored liqueur or 1 teaspoon orange extract			

Procedure

In a bowl, beat all ingredients until smooth. Store in the refrigerator.

Yield: 1 cup

Nutrition Facts

Nutrition (per serving): 25 calories, 10 calories from fat, 1.1g total fat, 3.5mg cholesterol, 18.6mg sodium, 11.5mg potassium, 2.9g carbohydrates, <1g fiber, 2.4g sugar, <1g protein.

George Washington married Martha Custis, widow of Colonel Daniel Parke Custis, on January 6, 1759.

1759: "I am now, I believe, fixed at this seat, with an agreeable partner for life; and I hope to find more happiness in retirement, than I ever experienced amidst the wide and bustling world."
George Washington

January, 1799: "To his equals he was condescending, to his inferiors kind, and to the dear object of his affections, exemplarily tender." General Henry Lee

December, 1799: On the night of his death, his attendants discovered on his breast, suspended by a ribbon, the miniature likeness of Mrs. Washington. He had worn it for more than forty years. (John Frederick Schroeder, 1854)

Pear Amber Jam

12 medium pears	10 oz. maraschino cherries
2 large oranges	6 cups granulated sugar
2 1/2 cups pineapple, drained	

Procedure

Wash and core pears. Cut pears fine. Wash oranges, cut and remove seeds. Grind orange and rind. In a large stainless bowl, mix cut pears, ground oranges, pineapple and cherries. Add 3/4 as much sugar as fruit (about 6 cups). Let stand overnight. Cook until thick and pears are clear, at least an hour. Ladle into hot, sterilized jars and process in hot water bath for 20 minutes.

Yield: Six pints

Nutrition Facts

Nutrition (per serving): 34 calories, <1 calories from fat, <1g total fat, 0mg cholesterol, <1mg sodium, 19.6mg potassium, 8.8g carbohydrates, <1g fiber, 7.7g sugar, <1g protein.

Cuppa Countess Comment:

Keeping Tea Fresh: stored properly, new crop premium teas will maintain high quality if stored in an airtight container at room temperature, away from light and humidity. Tea is like a sponge: it readily absorbs flavors and fragrances. That's good if you're buying jasmine-scented green tea and bad if you store an open tea package in your spice cabinet alongside onion and garlic powder.

Tea caddies or clamp-top porcelain jars are highly recommended.

Pumpkin Marmalade

6	cups diced sugar pumpkin	8	cups granulated sugar
3	whole lemons, peeled	1	cup steeped oolong tea
1	large orange, peeled	1/4 cup	apple juice
2"	piece fresh ginger, peeled and grated		

Procedure

Place pumpkin in a large, heavy-bottomed pot. Slice citrus very thin, removing seeds. Add citrus slices and sugar to pumpkin. Stir and leave overnight. Place over medium heat and stir in apple juice and tea water. Simmer uncovered 2 ½ hours or until thick. Pour into sterilized jars and seal.

Nutrition Facts

Nutrition (per serving): 67 calories, <1g calories from fat, <1g total fat, 0mg cholesterol, <1g sodium, 28 mg potassium, 17g carbohydrates, .05g fiber, 17g sugar, <1g protein.

"Exactly when the custom of drinking iced tea began is unknown, but it dates back at least to the 1860s, if not long before. A hot drink in vogue in the 1870s, tea a la Russe, made with sugar and sliced lemons, was also enjoyed cold. Iced tea was also available in the 1870s in hotels and on railroads." (Andrew F. Smith, 2004)

Rose Citrus Honey Butter

1	cup	butter, softened to room temperature	2	Tbs.	organic rose petals, shredded
1/2	cup	flax seed oil	2	Tbs.	crushed pineapple, drained
1/2	cup	honey	1	tsp.	pure vanilla extract
2	Tbs.	orange zest			

Procedure

In mixing bowl, hand blend until well mixed. Spread on scones, biscuits, muffins or use as a sandwich filling.

Yield: 4 cups

Nutrition Facts

Nutrition (per serving): 50 calories, 44 calories from fat, 5g total fat, 10.2mg cholesterol, <1mg sodium, 3.2mg potassium, 1.6g carbohydrates, <1g fiber, 1.5g sugar, <1g protein.

Cuppa Countess Comment: Although there are differing opinions about whether the honeybee is native to the Americas, conquering Spaniards in 1600 A.D. found native Mexicans and Central Americans had already developed beekeeping methods to produce honey for use in food and beverages. In the course of honey production, bees are vital for pollinating fruit and vegetable crops. The honey dispenser is always on my counter – ready for tea or toast.

Stone Fruit Chutney

1	cup	golden balsamic vinegar	2	tsp.	cardamom pods
1 1/2		cups sugar	1 1/2		tsp. peppercorns, crushed
2	lbs.	peaches, pitted	1/2 tsp.		anise seeds
2 1/2		lbs. apricot, plums or pluots, pitted	1/2 tsp.		fennel seeds
1	lb.	cherries, pitted	4		1" x 2" orange zest strips
2	tsp.	whole cloves	2		cinnamon sticks

Procedure

In a large stainless steel pot, stir together the vinegar and sugar. Blanch, peel and halve the peaches; remove the pits. Cut peach halves into thick slices, add to the pan along with the pitted apricots, and pitted cherries. Stir fruit to coat with the vinegar-sugar mixture.

Place the cloves, cardamom pods, peppercorns, anise seeds and fennel seeds on cheesecloth; tie with string to form a bag. Add spices, orange zest and cinnamon sticks to the pot. Let stand for 1 hour. Bring to a boil over medium heat. Reduce heat and simmer, uncovered, stirring occasionally, until the mixture thickens to jam-like consistency, about 1 hour and 15 minutes. Discard cloth bag and cinnamon sticks. Ladle hot chutney into sterilized jars. Process jars in a hot water bath for 15 minutes.

Yield: 7 half-pints

Nutrition Facts

Nutrition (per serving): 20 calories, <1 calories from fat, <1g total fat, 0mgcholesterol, <1mg sodium, 45.6mg potassium, 5.1g carbohydrates, <1g fiber, 4.3g sugar, <1g protein

Left to Right:
Edible Petal Butter
Blackberry, Lavender & Sage Jelly
Rice Flour Scones

All American Cream Scones

2 cups all-purpose flour	1 large egg, beaten
1/3 cup granulated sugar	1 tsp. pure vanilla extract
2 tsp. baking powder	1/2 cup heavy cream, plus 3 Tbs. for glaze
1/4 tsp. salt	
1/3 cup unsalted butter, cold	

Procedure

Preheat oven to 425°F.

In a large bowl, combine the flour, sugar, baking powder, and salt. Cut the butter into small pieces and blend into flour mixture to resemble coarse crumbs. Combine the whipping cream, beaten egg and vanilla. Add the liquid, stirring until the batter forms moist clumps. The batter will be sticky. Do not over mix.

Gather dough together with your hands and transfer to a lightly floured surface. Gently knead for about 10 seconds until dough forms a ball and is smooth. Pat dough into a 7-inch circle and 1 inch thick. Cut circle into 8 triangular sections. Brush off excess flour from scones on prepared baking sheet. Brush scones with cream and sprinkle lightly with sugar.

Bake for about 15 minutes or until lightly browned. Remove from oven. Transfer to a wire rack to cool.

Yield: 8 scones

Nutrition Facts

Nutrition (per serving): 276 calories, 124 calories from fat, 14.1g total fat, 67.1mg cholesterol, 210.7mg sodium, 56.4mg potassium, 33g carbohydrates, <1g fiber, 8.6g sugar, 4.4g protein.

Apple Cheddar Scones

1 1/2 cups all-purpose flour
1/2 cup toasted wheat germ
3 Tbs. sugar
2 tsp. baking powder
1/2 tsp. salt
2 Tbs. butter

1 Gala apple, cored and finely chopped
1/4 cup shredded cheddar cheese
1 large egg white, beaten
1/2 cup low fat (1%) milk

Procedure

Preheat oven to 400°F. Grease an 8-inch round cake pan.

In medium bowl, combine flour, wheat germ, sugar, baking powder, and salt. With pastry blender or fork, cut in butter until mixture is crumbly. Stir in apple and cheddar cheese.

Beat egg white and milk until combined. Add to flour mixture, mixing gently, until soft dough forms. Turn dough out onto lightly floured surface and knead 4 times.

Spread dough evenly in cake pan and score deeply with knife to make six wedges. Bake 25 to 30 minutes or until top springs back when gently pressed.

Yield: 6 scones

Nutrition Facts

Nutrition (per serving): 259 calories, 61 calories from fat, 7g total fat, 15.9mg cholesterol, 409.3mg sodium, 212.1mg potassium, 42.1g carbohydrates, 3g fiber, 10.4g sugar, 8.2g protein.

Apple Date Scones

1/3	cup	cold butter	1/2 cup	rolled oats
1 1/2		cups all-purpose flour	1/2 cup	apple; unpeeled -- chopped
2	Tbs.	granulated sugar	1/4 cup	chopped dates
2	tsp.	baking powder	1	large egg, beaten
1/2	tsp.	ground cinnamon	1/3 cup	half and half
1/4	tsp.	salt		

Procedure

Preheat oven to 400°F.

Cut the butter into the flour, sugar, baking powder, cinnamon, and salt with a pastry blender in a large bowl until the mixture resembles fine crumbs. Stir in the oats, apple, and dates. Stir in the egg and just enough half-and-half so that the dough leaves the side of the bowl and forms a ball.

Turn the dough onto a lightly floured surface; gently roll in flour to coat. Knead lightly 10 times. Pat or roll into an 8-inch circle on an ungreased cookie sheet. Score (mark) the top into 8 sections. Brush with half-and-half and sprinkle with sugar.

Bake for 16 to 18 minutes, or until golden brown. Immediately remove from the cookie sheet; carefully separate the wedges. Serve warm.

Yield: 8 scones

Nutrition Facts

Nutrition (per serving): 228 calories, 88 calories from fat, 10g total fat, 50.5mg cholesterol, 262.8mg sodium, 112.4mg potassium, 30.6g carbohydrates, 1.8g fiber, 7.7g sugar, 4.6g protein.

Apricot Scones

4	cups	all-purpose flour	2	Tbs. orange peel -- grated
1/2	cup	granulated sugar	1	cup dried apricots
4	tsp.	baking powder	1	whole egg
1	tsp.	salt	1	cup heavy cream
1/2	tsp.	cream of tartar	1/2	cup orange juice
3/4	cup	butter		Cream and granulated sugar

Procedure

Preheat oven to 425°F. Grease a large baking sheet.

In a large bowl, combine the flour, sugar, baking powder, salt, and cream of tartar. Cut in the butter until the mixture resembles coarse crumbs. Add the orange peel and apricots or dates. In a small bowl, beat together the egg, cream, and orange juice.

Add to the dry ingredients and mix lightly with a fork until a soft dough forms. Turn the dough out onto a lightly floured surface and knead gently 5 or 6 times. Divide the dough into quarters and roll each to a 1/2-inch thickness. Cut into wedges. Place the scones on the prepared baking sheet. Brush with cream and sprinkle with sugar. Bake for 15 to 18 minutes.

Yield: 18 scones

Nutrition Facts

Nutrition (per serving): 264 calories, 117 calories from fat, 13.4g total fat, 50.8mg cholesterol, 249.6mg sodium, 161mg potassium, 33g carbohydrates, 1.4g fiber, 10.1g sugar, 3.9g protein.

Apricot White Chocolate Scones

2	cups	all-purpose flour	1		large egg, beaten
1/3	cup	granulated sugar	1 1/2	tsp.	vanilla extract
2	tsp.	baking powder	6	oz.	white chocolate chips
1/2	tsp.	salt	1	cup	toasted coarsely chopped pecans
1/4	cup	unsalted butter, cold	1	cup	finely chopped dried apricots
1/2	cup	heavy whipping cream			

Procedure

Preheat oven to 425° F.

In a large bowl, sift together the flour, sugar, baking powder, and salt. Cut the butter into 1/2 inch cubes and distribute them over the flour mixture. With a pastry blender or two knives used scissors fashion, cut in the butter until the mixture resembles coarse crumbs. In a small bowl, stir together the cream, egg, and vanilla. Add the cream mixture to the flour mixture and knead until combined. Knead in the white chocolate, pecans, and apricots.

With lightly floured hands, pat the dough out on a floured work surface to a thickness of 5/8 inch. Cut circles in the dough with a biscuit cutter. Bake scones on ungreased baking sheet for 15 to 20 minutes, or until lightly browned on top.

Yield: 8 or 9 scones

Nutrition Facts

Nutrition (per serving): 441 calories, 212 calories from fat, 25g total fat, 55.2mg cholesterol, 255.5mg sodium, 344.2mg potassium, 52.2g carbohydrates, 2.7g fiber, 15.7g sugar, 7.2g protein.

Bacon Cornmeal Scones

2	cups all-purpose flour		1/2 tsp.	salt
2	cups yellow cornmeal		2/3 cup	vegetable shortening
4	tsp. baking powder		8	each bacon slices; cooked and crumbled
1	Tbs. sugar			
1/2 tsp.	baking soda		1 1/3	cups buttermilk

Procedure

Preheat oven to 425° F.; grease a large baking sheet.

In a large bowl, sift together flour, cornmeal, baking powder, sugar, baking soda, and salt. Cut in the shortening until mixture resembles coarse crumbs. Reserve 2 tablespoons crumbled bacon. Add buttermilk and remaining bacon to dry ingredients; mix with a fork until mixture forms soft dough.

Turn dough out onto a lightly floured surface and knead gently 5 or 6 times. Divide dough into thirds. With a lightly floured rolling pin, roll each third of the dough into a 7-inch round; cut into 4 wedges. Place scones one inch apart on prepared pan. Pierce tops with the tines of a fork. Brush tops with water and sprinkle with reserved bacon.

Bake for 15 to 18 minutes, or until golden brown.

Yield: 12 scones

Nutrition Facts

Nutrition (per serving): 297 calories, 133 calories from fat, 14.8g total fat, 13.3mg cholesterol, 402.9mg sodium, 152.2mg potassium, 34.4g carbohydrates, 2.1g fiber, 2.5g sugar, 6.7g protein.

Basil Bran Scones

1 1/4	cups	all-purpose flour up to 1 1/2 cups flour	1	tsp.	dried basil
3	Tbs.	oat bran	1/2	tsp.	salt
2	Tbs.	grated parmesan cheese	1	cup	whipping cream
2	tsp.	baking powder	1	tsp.	oat bran

Procedure

Preheat oven to 425° F. Grease a cookie sheet.

In a large bowl, combine 1 1/4 cups flour, 3 tablespoons oat bran, cheese, baking powder, basil and salt; blend well. Reserve 1 teaspoon whipping cream. Add the remaining cream to the flour mixture, stirring just until a soft dough forms. If the dough is too wet, stir in additional flour, one tablespoon at a time.

On a floured surface, gently knead the dough to form a smooth ball. Place on the cookie sheet; pat or roll into a 6-inch circle. Score into 8 wedges; do not separate. Brush with the reserved whipping cream; sprinkle with one teaspoon of oat bran.

Bake for 15 to 18 minutes, or until lightly browned. Cut into wedges; serve warm.

Yield: 8 scones

Nutrition Facts

Nutrition (per serving): 186 calories, 103 calories from fat, 11.7g total fat, 41.9mg cholesterol, 298.2mg sodium, 64.9mg potassium, 17.8g carbohydrates, <1g fiber, <1g sugar, 3.6g protein.

Blueberry Lemon Drop Scones

2	cup	all-purpose flour
1/3	cup	sugar
2	tsp.	baking powder
1/2	tsp.	baking soda
1/4	tsp.	salt
8	oz.	carton lemon yogurt
1	each	egg, lightly beaten
1/4	cup	butter, melted

1	tsp.	grated lemon peel
1	cup	fresh or frozen blueberries

Glaze

1	cup	confectioners' sugar
1	Tbs.	lemon juice
1	tsp.	grated lemon peel

Procedure

Preheat oven to 400 degrees F. Grease a cookie sheet. In a large bowl, sift together the dry ingredients. Combine yogurt, egg, butter, and lemon peel; stir into dry ingredients just until moistened. Fold in blueberries. Drop by tablespoonsful onto a baking sheet. Bake for 15-18 minutes or until lightly browned.

Glaze

Combine confectioners' sugar, lemon juice, and grated lemon peel; drizzle over warm scones.

Yield: Two dozen small drop scones

Nutrition Facts

Nutrition (per serving): 81 calories, 21 calories from fat, 2.4g total fat, 14.4mg cholesterol, 100.8mg sodium, 41.1mg potassium, 13.2g carbohydrates, <1g fiber, 3.6g sugar, 1.9g protein.

Cuppa Countess Comment: "Labor to keep alive in your breast that little celestial fire called conscience." ~ George Washington

Blueberry Nonfat Scones

3   cups whole wheat pastry flour, sifted
1 1/4 cups white cornmeal
1 1/4 cups fructose sugar
1   Tbs. baking powder
1   tsp. baking soda
1/2 tsp. salt

1 1/2 cups nonfat sour cream
1/2 cup   prune puree
1/2 Tbs. butter extract
1   tsp. vanilla extract
8   oz.   frozen blueberries

Procedure

Preheat oven to 350°F. Spray a baking sheet with non-stick cooking spray.

Measure frozen blueberries and put into a small bowl. Toss berries with a handful of cornmeal to prevent batter discoloration and return to freezer until ready to use.

Combine dry ingredients in a large mixing bowl. Add wet ingredients and mix with a wooden spoon. When thoroughly combined, fold in blueberries.

Drop dough by half-cup measure onto baking sheet. Flatten scones slightly. Garnish the center of each scone with a few blueberries and dust with a sprinkle of cornmeal.

Bake 20 minutes or until golden brown.

Yield: 18-24 scones

Nutrition Facts

Nutrition (per serving): 127 calories, 4 calories from fat, <1g total fat, <1mg cholesterol, 175.2mg sodium, 103.7mg potassium, 28.7g carbohydrates, 2.7g fiber, 8.1g sugar, 3.1g protein.

Blueberry Oat Scones

1 1/2	cups oat bran		1/2 cup	butter
1 1/2	cups all-purpose flour		2	large eggs, beaten
1/3 cup	light brown sugar -- packed		1/3 cup	plain yogurt
2 tsp.	baking powder		1 tsp.	vanilla extract
1 tsp.	cream of tartar		1 1/2 cups blueberries	

Procedure

Preheat oven to 400° F.; grease a baking sheet.

In a large bowl, mix the bran, flour, sugar, baking powder, and cream of tartar together. Cut in the butter. In a separate bowl, mix the eggs, yogurt, and vanilla extract. Blend into the dry ingredients. Carefully fold in the blueberries. Pat into a circle on the baking sheet. Cut into wedges, wiping the knife each time.

Bake for 20 to 25 minutes or until lightly browned.

Yield: 12 scones

Nutrition Facts

Nutrition (per serving): 206 calories, 85 calories from fat, 9.6g total fat, 56mg cholesterol, 102.2mg sodium, 189.6mg potassium, 29.2g carbohydrates, 2.7g fiber, 8.5g sugar, 5.3g protein.

Blueberry Scones, Traditional

2	tsp. flour	1/4 tsp.	salt
1	tsp. cinnamon	1/3 cup	butter
1	cup blueberries	2	large eggs, beaten
1 3/4 cups flour		3 to 4 Tbs.	heavy cream
1	Tbs. baking powder	2 Tbs.	milk
1/4 cup sugar			Cinnamon sugar

Procedure

Preheat oven to 400 degrees F. Mix 2 tsp. flour, cinnamon, and blueberries together gently and set aside. Sift together the flour, baking powder, sugar and salt; cut in butter. Break eggs into measuring cup; beat with fork. Add enough cream to make 2/3 cup liquid. Lightly stir egg mixture and berries into dry ingredients. Handle dough as little as possible. Turn dough out onto floured board; divide into two portions. Place on ungreased baking sheet; pat each dough portion into a 6-inch circle, 3/4 inch thick. Cut into 6 wedges. Brush with milk and cinnamon sugar. Bake for about 15 minutes or until lightly browned.

Yield: 12 wedge-type scones

Nutrition Facts

Nutrition (per serving): 168 calories, 67 calories from fat, 7.6g total fat, 54.1mg cholesterol, 185.7mg sodium, 49.9mg potassium, 22g carbohydrates, <1g fiber, 6.7g sugar, 3.3g protein.

Boston Back Bay Scones

2 cups self-rising flour, sifted

1/4 cup butter, cold and diced small

1/2 tsp. baking soda

3/4 cup buttermilk

milk or egg for glaze, if desired

Procedure

Preheat oven to 350°F. Lightly grease a baking sheet.

Put self-rising flour into medium mixing bowl. Into flour, work in cold, diced butter to resemble coarse crumbs. Stir soda into buttermilk until it begins to foam. Make a well in the center of the flour. Pour buttermilk mixture into well and stir with fork incorporating just enough flour to make a very soft dough. Gather into ball and place on lightly floured board. Pat or roll into a circle, kneading very lightly. Use spatula to cut into 8 or 10 wedges. Transfer to greased baking sheet.

To give scones a shine, brush with milk. For a golden shine, brush wedges with an egg yolk beaten with a tablespoon of water. Bake 10 to 12 minutes.

Yield: 10 scones

Nutrition Facts

Nutrition (per serving): 185 calories, 89 calories from fat, 10.1g total fat, 46.3mg cholesterol, 408mg sodium, 68.2mg potassium, 19.5g carbohydrates, <1g fiber, <1g sugar, 3.8g protein.

Bran Date Scones

3	cups	self-rising flour, sifted	1	tsp.	mixed ground spices
1	cup	bran	1/4	cup	butter or margarine
2	Tbs.	brown sugar, packed	2	Tbs.	honey
1/2	cup	chopped dates	1	cup	milk plus additional milk

Procedure

Preheat oven to 425° F.

In a large bowl, combine the flour, bran, brown sugar, dates and spices. In a small saucepan, combine the butter, honey, and milk. Melt butter; pour into the dry ingredients.

Turn onto a floured surface and knead lightly. Roll the dough to about 1/2-inch thick. Cut out the scones using a 2 1/2-inch round cutter. Place the scones on a baking sheet and brush with milk.

Bake for 12 to 14 minutes, or until golden brown.

Yield: 18-24 scones

Nutrition Facts

Nutrition (per serving): 107 calories, 22 calories from fat, 2.6g total fat, 5.9mg cholesterol, 203.6mg sodium, 87mg potassium, 20.1g carbohydrates, 1.4g fiber, 5.5g sugar, 2.7g protein.

Buckingham Palace Scones

3 1/2 cups flour
1/2 cup sugar
1/8 tsp. salt
1 Tbs. baking powder

3/4 cup butter
1 large egg, beaten
1/2 cup milk
1/2 cup raisins

Procedure

Preheat oven to 350°F. Lightly grease a baking sheet.

Sift together the flour, sugar, salt, and baking powder. Using a pastry blender, cut the butter into the flour mixture until crumbly. Add sugar and raisins.

Make a well in center of the mixture; add egg and small amount of milk. If mixture appears to be too dry, add more milk. Blend to a smooth dough. Roll out on floured board to 1/2 inch thick. Use 2-inch cutter with fluted edge. Place on lightly greased baking sheet, brush with beaten egg.

Bake in 350°F oven for 15 minutes or until golden brown.

Yield: 18 scones

Nutrition Facts

Nutrition (per serving): 199 calories, 73 calories from fat, 8.3g total fat, 32.6mg cholesterol, 106.1mg sodium, 76.8mg potassium, 28.3g carbohydrates, <1g fiber, 8.7g sugar, 3.3g protein.

Buttery Currant Scones

2 cups all-purpose flour

2 Tbs. sugar

1 Tbs. baking powder

1/4 tsp. salt

1/2 cup vegetable shortening

1/2 cup currants

1 large egg, beaten

1 cup half-and-half

Extra flour for kneading

Procedure

Preheat oven to 425° F.

Sift together dry ingredients. Cut the shortening into dry ingredients until mixture resembles coarse cornmeal. Stir in currants. Stir the beaten egg into the half-and-half cream. Make a well in center of mixture and add the egg/cream mixture. Stir with fork until blended.

Form dough into a ball and place on a lightly floured surface. Knead lightly with fingertips 10-15 times. Pat or roll dough into a 1/2" thick circle. Cut into 12 wedges and transfer to an ungreased baking sheet.

Bake 15-20 minutes or until golden brown.

Yield: 12 triangular scones

Nutrition Facts

Nutrition (per serving): 249 calories, 104 calories from fat, 11.6g total fat, 29.9mg cholesterol, 185.6mg sodium, 119mg potassium, 31.6g carbohydrates, 1.3g fiber, 6.3g sugar, 4.6g protein.

Cape Breton Scones

2 cups flour, plus 1/4 cup reserved flour	1 cup raisins or currants
2 Tbs. sugar	1/2 cup sour cream
1 Tbs. baking powder	1/4 cup oil
1 tsp. salt	1 large egg, lightly beaten
1/4 tsp. baking soda	3 Tbs. milk

Procedure

Preheat oven to 425°F. Lightly spray cookie sheet with non-stick cooking spray.

Sift together flour, sugar, baking powder, salt, and baking soda. Stir in the raisins or currants. Mix the remaining ingredients and stir into the flour mixture. Stir until the dough is evenly moistened.

Put the 1/4 cup reserved flour onto a working surface. Turn the dough onto the lightly floured surface and knead lightly until no longer sticky. Do not overwork the dough.

Divide the dough into halves then pat each ball of dough into a 6" circle with the top slightly rounded. Brush the tops with milk and sprinkle with sugar. Cut each circle into 6 wedges. Place 2 inches apart on a prepared cookie sheet.

Bake at 425°F for 10 to 12 minutes or until golden brown.

Yield: 12 triangular scones

Nutrition Facts

Nutrition (per serving): 197 calories, 57 calories from fat, 6.5g total fat, 21.9mg cholesterol, 355.6mg sodium, 152.7mg potassium, 31.8g carbohydrates, 1.1g fiber, 10.5g sugar, 3.8g protein.

Chocolate Scones

2 1/4   cups all-purpose flour
1/4 cup   whole wheat flour
2   Tbs. granulated sugar
1   Tbs. baking powder
1/2 tsp.   salt
1   tsp. ground cinnamon

1/2 cup   butter
1   large egg, beaten
1/2 cup   milk plus extra
1/2 cup   mini chocolate chips
          Egg whites or heavy cream

Procedure

Preheat oven to 400° F.

In a large bowl, combine the flours, sugar, baking powder, salt and cinnamon; mix well. Cut the butter into the flour mixture until it resembles small peas. Break the egg into a 1-cup measure and add milk to make 2/3 cup.

Add the milk, egg and chocolate morsels to the flour mixture and combine lightly until a loose ball is formed. Lightly knead the mixture in the bowl 5 to 10 times and then break into 2 equal portions. Press down each ball on an ungreased cookie sheet to form a 6-inch circle. Score each circle into 6 wedges. Brush with a wash of egg whites or heavy cream.

Bake for 15 to 20 minutes.

Yield: 12 scones

Nutrition Facts

Nutrition (per serving): 186 calories, 76 calories from fat, 8.7g total fat, 38.9mg cholesterol, 230.8mg sodium, 52.2mg potassium, 23.4g carbohydrates, <1g fiber, 3.1g sugar, 3.7g protein.

Cinnamon Chocolate Scones

4	cups	self-rising flour
1	tsp.	ground cinnamon
1/2	cup	butter, cold and cut into small chunks

1 1/4 cups milk

1/2 cup lavender honey

1 1/2 cups semi-sweet chocolate chunks

Procedure

Preheat oven to 375 degrees F. Coat a cookie sheet with cooking spray. In a bowl, mix flour and cinnamon together. Cut in the butter pieces. Add milk and honey and mix well. Turn dough out onto a floured working surface, sprinkle with chocolate chunks and knead gently for five or six turns to work in the chocolate pieces.

Roll out dough to 1/2 in. and cut into shapes. Transfer to baking sheet and bake for 15 minutes or until lightly browned.

Yield: 24 scones

Nutrition Facts

Nutrition (per serving): 186 calories, 63 calories from fat, 7.4g total fat, 11.2mg cholesterol, 271.8mg sodium, 50.2mg potassium, 28.6g carbohydrates, 1.3g fiber, 6.5g sugar, 3g protein.

Colonial Cranberry Scones

3	cups	all-purpose flour	1 tsp.	grated orange zest
1/3	cup	sugar	1 cup	buttermilk
2 1/2		tsp. baking powder	**Glaze:**	
1/2	tsp.	baking soda	1 Tbs.	heavy cream
3/4	tsp.	salt	1/4 tsp.	ground cinnamon
3/4	cup	chilled margarine, cut into 6 to 8 pieces	2 Tbs.	sugar
3/4	cup	dried cranberries		

Procedure

Preheat oven to 400° F. Lightly grease a baking sheet.

In a large bowl, sift flour, sugar, baking powder, baking soda, and salt. Add the margarine and beat mix until well blended. Add the dried cranberries and orange zest. Pour in the buttermilk and mix until blended. Gather the dough into a ball and divide in half. On a lightly floured board, roll into 2 circles approximately 1/2- to 3/4-inch thick. Cut each circle into 8 wedges.

To make the glaze, combine the cream, cinnamon and sugar in a small bowl. Set aside. Bake the scones at 400°F on the prepared baking sheet for 12 to 15 minutes or until they are golden. Remove scones from oven and brush with glaze. Serve with Cranberry Butter.

Yield: 16 scones

Nutrition Facts

Nutrition (per serving): 327 calories, 124 calories from fat, 14g total fat, 16mg cholesterol, 385.8mg sodium, 68.3mg potassium, 47.6g carbohydrates, 2.5g fiber, 6.5g sugar, 3.1g protein.

Coombe Castle Scones

2	cups self-rising flour		1 1/4	cup milk, approximately
1/4 cup	margarine or butter		1/4 tsp.	salt
3 oz.	sugar			

Procedure

Preheat oven to 425° Fahrenheit.

Mix flour, sugar and salt in a large bowl. Rub margarine or butter into the dry ingredients and add enough milk for a firm dough. Roll out mixture to approximately 1 inch thick and cut with a 2 1/2 inch pastry cutter into circles. Glaze with milk and bake at 425°F for 10 minutes. Remove and cool.

Yield: 12 scones

Nutrition Facts

Nutrition (per serving): 165 calories, 57 calories from fat, 6.4g total fat, 8.3mg cholesterol, 387.1mg sodium, 66.7mg potassium, 23.8g carbohydrates, <1g fiber, 8.4g sugar, 3g protein.

In Devon and Cornwall - the traditional home in southwest England of cream teas - there is still a debate on whether the jam or the cream should be put on the scone first. History would probably support the cream spread first as a replacement for butter in the farmhouses where it was available every day. However, we recommend spreading the jam first and topping it with cream to better represent the proportions of the sweet jam and the cream while making for a more attractive presentation (no "got jam" grins).

Cranberry Cherry Scones

2 1/2 cups all-purpose flour	1/2 cup nonfat plain yogurt
3 Tbs. cornstarch	2 Tbs. canola oil
1 Tbs. baking powder	1/2 cup skim milk
1 tsp. salt	1/3 cup granulated sugar
1/4 tsp. ground cinnamon	1/2 cup each dried cranberries and dried
2 Tbs. cold unsalted butter	cherries, finely chopped
1 large egg or 1/4 cup liquid egg substitute	

Procedure

Preheat oven to 425°F. Line a baking sheet with parchment paper.

In a large mixing bowl, sift together the flour, cornstarch, baking powder, salt, and cinnamon. Using a pastry blender or your fingers, work in the butter to size of small peas. In another large bowl, whisk together egg, yogurt, oil, milk, and sugar, reserving 1 tablespoon of sugar. Add the flour mixture, cranberries and cherries. Mix until just combined. Do not over mix.

Drop by heaping spoonsful into 12 mounds onto prepared baking sheet. Sprinkle with reserved tablespoon of granulated sugar.

Bake for 12 to 15 minutes or until golden.

Yield: 12 drop scones

Nutrition Facts

Nutrition (per serving): 273 calories, 56 calories from fat, 6.4g total fat, 26.9mg cholesterol, 364.6mg sodium, 74.7mg potassium, 48.8g carbohydrates, 2.4g fiber, 5.7g sugar, 5.1g protein.

Cranberry Orange Scones

2	cups	flour	1/2	cup	heavy cream
1	Tbs.	sugar	1	large	egg
2	tsp.	baking powder	1	cup	CRAISINS® Sweetened Dried Cranberries
1/2	tsp.	salt			
1/4	cup	butter or margarine	2	tsp.	orange zest
					Sugar

Procedure

Preheat oven to 425° F. Grease a cookie sheet.

Combine dry ingredients in a large mixing bowl. Work butter or margarine into dry ingredients until butter is the size of small peas. Add remaining ingredients and mix just until dry ingredients are moist. Turn dough onto a lightly floured surface and gather into a ball. Pat into a circle 3/4-inch thick; cut into wedges. Place on cookie sheet. Sprinkle with sugar.

Bake 12 minutes or until golden brown.

Yield: 8 scones

Nutrition Facts

Nutrition (per serving): 277 calories, 109 calories from fat, 12.4g total fat, 62.1mg cholesterol, 283.4mg sodium, 61.1mg potassium, 38.2g carbohydrates, 1.6g fiber, 11.4g sugar, 4.4g protein.

Cranberry Walnut Scones

2	cups flour	1/2	cup	cranberries, chopped, (fresh or dried)
1/4	cup maple sugar			
2	tsp. baking powder	1/4	cup	walnuts, chopped
2	Tbs. unsalted butter	1	cup	buttermilk
		1	Tbs.	non-fat milk

Procedure

Preheat oven to 425 degrees F. Spray baking sheet with cooking spray.

In a large bowl, sift together flour, sugar, baking powder, and salt. Cut in butter. Stir in cranberries and walnuts. Make a well in center and stir in buttermilk. Dough will be sticky. Pat into an 8" round; score into 8 sections. Brush top with milk and sprinkle with sugar. Bake for 14 to 18 minutes or until golden brown.

Yield: 8 large scones

Nutrition Facts

Nutrition (per serving): 331 calories, 56 calories from fat, 6.4g total fat, 8.9mg cholesterol, 237.8mg sodium, 150.5mg potassium, 62.5g carbohydrates, 3.5g fiber, 5.5g sugar, 6.1g protein.

Cuppa Countess Tea Scones

5 cups self-rising flour	Additional cold milk
1/2 cup sugar	Additional butter
3 large eggs (cold), beaten	Extra Self-Rising Flour
1 pint heavy whipping cream (cold)	

Procedure

Preheat oven to 425 degrees F. Lightly spray a baking sheet (do not use an "Air Bake"). Into a large bowl, sift the flour and sugar. In a 4-cup measuring cup, lightly beat the eggs. Add the whipping cream to the eggs. Add enough milk to make 3 cups liquid. Make a well in the center of the dry ingredients and add the liquid, stirring with a wooden spoon until the batter forms moist clumps. The batter will be sticky.

Transfer dough to a generously floured surface. Gently knead until dough forms a ball. Incorporate additional self-rising flour (up to 3/4 cup) to form a smooth ball. Roll dough to 1/2" thickness. Cut out scones with a 2" round or shaped cookie cutter. Dip cookie cutter in additional flour to help release scones between cuts. Bake for approximately 18 minutes, until lightly browned. Makes about 28-42 scones depending upon cookie cutter size. Note: See scone variations.

Yield: 28 to 42 medium size scones

Scone Variations:

To the Cuppa Countess Scone Basic Recipe, revise as follows:

Candied Ginger Scones: Add 1 tsp. Ginger spice to dry ingredients and one cup minced candied ginger to dough before kneading.

Chocolate Chip Scones: Add 1 tsp. Cinnamon to dry ingredients, 1 Tbs.. Butter Flavor to milk mixture and add 2 cups chocolate chips to dough before kneading.

Earl Grey Scones: Add grated rind of one orange and contents of two Earl Grey teabags to the dry ingredients.

Heathman Scones: Add 1 Tbs.. caramel flavoring to the milk mixture; fold in two crushed Heath candy bars to dough before kneading.

Illusive Lemon Spice Scones: Add 1 tsp. Cardamom, 1 tsp. Mace and zest of two lemons to the dry ingredients.

Lemon Thyme Scones: Reduce sugar to 1/4 cup. Add 1/2 cup minced fresh thyme (lemon or pineapple thyme if you have it) and zest of two lemons to the dry ingredients. Use juice of the lemons as part of the 3 cups of liquid.

Orange Pecan Scones: As part of the 3 cups liquid, add 1/2 cup orange liqueur or orange juice; add zest of two oranges and 1 cup finely chopped pecans to the dry ingredients.

Vanilla Cherry Scones: As part of the 3 cups liquid, add 2 tsp. vanilla extract and 1/4 c. Kirsch or 1 tsp. almond extract; add 1 tsp. Mace and 1 cup finely chopped candied cherries to the dry ingredients.

Zesty Cheddar Scones: (not for the faint of heart) Reduce sugar to 2 Tbs..; as part of the 3 cups liquid, add 2 Tbs.. Worcestershire sauce; add 1 Tbs.. crushed chili pepper to the dry ingredients; fold 2 cups grated cheddar cheese into the dough before kneading.

Cuppa Countess Comment: This is the basic scone recipe that I used at Carnelian Rose Tea's Chandelier Room and for catering - it offers so much flexibility. Never able to pass a cookie-cutter display without checking for new shapes, cookie cutters inspire me to add different ingredients.
The perfect scone is a serious matter to daily imbibers and they are such a simple treat to make!

Currant Scones

1/2 cup dried currants
1/4 cup apricot brandy
2 cup all-purpose flour
3 tsp. baking powder
1/2 tsp. salt
1 Tbs. sugar
1/4 cup butter

1 Tbs. orange zest
3/4 cup half-and-half cream

Topping

1 whole egg, beaten, mixed with 4 Tbs. milk
1/2 cup brown sugar

Procedure

Soak currants in brandy for 1/2 hour to plump. Drain and set aside.

Preheat oven to 425 degrees F. Lightly grease a baking sheet. Into a medium mixing bowl, sift together the flour, baking powder, sugar and salt. Using a pastry blender, cut in butter until mixture resembles coarse meal. Add currants and orange zest. Stir in half-and-half, using a fork, until dry ingredients are moistened.

Turn dough out onto a floured surface and knead six times. Roll out to 3/4-inch thickness; cut with a small biscuit cutter. Place rounds on baking sheet. Brush with egg glaze, then sprinkle with brown sugar. Bake for 15 minutes or until sugar has caramelized and tops are golden brown.

Yield: 24 scones

Nutrition Facts

Nutrition (per serving): 97 calories, 27 calories from fat, 3.1g total fat, 16.7mg cholesterol, 117.9mg sodium, 67.6mg potassium, 15.7g carbohydrates, <1g fiber, 7g sugar, 1.7g protein.

Date Scones

1 1/2	cup	all-purpose flour	2	tsp.	cinnamon
1/2 cup	whole wheat flour	1/4 cup	brown sugar
1/4 cup	oat bran	1/2 cup	unsalted butter, cold
2 tsp.	baking powder	1	whole egg, beaten
1/2 tsp.	baking soda	2/3 cup	buttermilk
1 tsp.	salt	2/3 cup	chopped dates

Procedure

Preheat oven to 350 degrees F. Combine the all-purpose and whole wheat flours, the bran, baking powder, soda, salt, cinnamon and brown sugar. Cut in the butter. Add the egg, buttermilk and dates; do not over mix. (If the dough seems too sticky to work with, add a couple more tablespoons flour.) Shape the dough into a rectangle about 1 inch thick on a floured surface. Cut into 12 triangles. Place on an ungreased baking sheet and bake about 25 minutes.

Yield: 12 scones

Nutrition Facts

Nutrition (per serving): 207 calories, 76 calories from fat, 8.6g total fat, 38.5mg cholesterol, 351.2mg sodium, 144.6mg potassium, 30.3g carbohydrates, 1.9g fiber, 11.5g sugar, 3.8g protein.

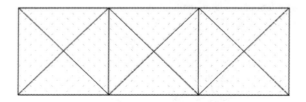

Dilly Cheese Scones

2 1/2	cups all-purpose flour	2	tsp. dill weed
1/2 cup	(2 oz.) shredded cheddar cheese	1/2 tsp.	salt
1/2 cup	(2 oz.) shredded Swiss cheese	3/4 cup	butter or margarine
1/4 cup	chopped fresh parsley	2	whole eggs, slightly beaten
1	Tbs. baking powder	1/2 cup	half-and-half

Procedure

Heat oven to 400 degrees F. Lightly spray a cookie sheet with non-stick cooking spray.

Sift together the flour, baking powder, and dill weed. Stir in the fresh parsley and shredded cheeses. Cut in the butter until crumbly. Stir in eggs and half-and-half just until moistened. Turn the dough onto lightly floured surface and knead until smooth. Do not over mix. Divide dough in half. Roll each half into an 8" circle. Cut each circle into 8 pie-shaped wedges and place 1" apart on a prepared cookie sheet. Bake for 15 to 20 minutes or until lightly browned.

Yield: 16 scones

Nutrition Facts

Nutrition (per serving): 197 calories, 111 calories from fat, 12.6g total fat, 59.6mg cholesterol, 208.1mg sodium, 57.8mg potassium, 15.9g carbohydrates, <1g fiber, <1g sugar, 5.2g protein.

Dilly Cheese Scones are luscious as a savory treat with salmon mousse or lemon curd. Dilly Cheese Scones pair nicely with Keemun or a brisk Kenya tea.

Drop Griddle Scones

1	cup	all-purpose flour	2	Tbs.	granulated sugar
1	tsp.	cream of tartar	1		whole large egg
1/2	tsp.	baking soda	1	cup	milk
1/2	tsp.	salt	1	Tbs.	vegetable oil

Procedure

Use griddle or heavy frying pan. Sift the dry ingredients together into a mixing bowl and make a well in the center. Add the egg and half the milk and mix to a smooth batter. Gradually beat in the remaining milk with the oil. Heat a heavy frying pan or griddle and grease lightly. Drop tablespoons of the batter onto the hot surface and cook until the top is blistered. Turn with a spatula and cook until the underside is golden brown. Serve with butter and jam or marmalade.

Nutrition Facts

Nutrition (per serving): 73 calories, 19 calories from fat, 2.1g total fat, 19.3mg cholesterol, 163.8mg sodium, 88.5mg potassium, 11.2g carbohydrates, <1g fiber, 3.2g sugar, 2.3g protein.

Cuppa Countess Comment:
The Virtuous Woman~ "She watches over the ways of her household, and does not eat the bread of idleness. Her children rise up and call her blessed." Proverbs 31:27-28a

Fort Washington Tea Scones

4 cups all-purpose flour	2/3 cup butter
2 Tbs. sugar	1 1/3 cup half and half
4 tsp. baking powder	1 whole large egg
1 tsp. salt	1/4 cup golden raisins, optional
1/2 tsp. cream of tartar	

Procedure

Preheat oven to 425 degrees F. Grease a large baking sheet.

In a large bowl, combine flour, sugar, baking powder, salt and cream of tartar. With a pastry blender or two knives, cut in the butter until the mixture resembles coarse crumbs. In a small bowl, beat together the half-and-half and egg. Reserve 2 tablespoons of the milk-egg mixture. Add remaining mixture to dry ingredients along with the raisins. Mix lightly with a fork until mixture clings together and forms a soft dough.

Turn dough out onto a lightly floured surface and knead gently 5 or 6 times. Divide dough in half. With a lightly floured rolling pin, roll one-half of the dough into a 7-inch round; cut into 4 wedges. Repeat with remaining dough. Place scones one inch apart on prepared pan. Pierce tops with the tines of a fork. Brush tops with reserved egg mixture. Bake for 15 to 18 minutes or until golden brown.

Yield: 8 large scones

Nutrition Facts

Nutrition (per serving): 452 calories, 187 calories from fat, 21.2g total fat, 82.1mg cholesterol, 563.7mg sodium, 197.6mg potassium, 57g carbohydrates, 1.9g fiber, 6.1g sugar, 8.8g protein.

Frangelico Currant Scones

4 1/2	cups all-purpose flour		1	cup currants
2	tsp. baking powder		3	Tbs. Frangelico Liqueur
1/2 tsp.	baking soda			**Glaze**
3	Tbs. sugar		1	whole egg, beaten
1/4 tsp.	salt		1/4 cup	light cream
1/2 cup	unsalted butter, cold			
1 1/4	cup heavy cream			

Procedure

Preheat oven to 375 degrees F. Lightly grease a baking sheet. Soak currants in Frangelico to soften - about thirty minutes. Dice the butter and put into food processor. Add half the flour and process slightly; add remaining flour and process until mixture resembles coarse meal. Transfer to a bowl and add cream slowly mixing until dough just holds together. Add currants and mix gently. Flatten into a round and wrap in plastic. Chill for 30 minutes.

Roll dough into a circle 1/2-inch thick. Using a biscuit cutter, cut the dough into various shapes. Place scones onto prepared baking sheet. Beat egg and light cream in a bowl and brush the tops of scones with mixture. Bake 13 to 15 minutes or until golden brown. Makes 24 to 50 scones depending on cutter size.

Yield: 50

Nutrition Facts

Nutrition (per serving): 96 calories, 39 calories from fat, 4.5g total fat, 18.1mg cholesterol, 42.8mg sodium, 45.6mg potassium, 12.1g carbohydrates, <1g fiber, 2.7g sugar, 1.6g protein.

Fruit and Oat Scones

1 1/2 cup all-purpose flour

1 1/4 cup rolled oats

1/4 cup sugar

1   Tbs. baking powder

1/4 tsp. salt (optional)

1/3 cup   margarine

6   oz.   package diced dried mixed fruit

1/2 cup   milk

1   whole egg, lightly beaten

Topping

1   tsp.   sugar

1/8 tsp.   cinnamon

Procedure

Heat oven to 375 degrees F. Lightly grease baking sheet. Combine flour, oats, sugar, baking powder, and salt. Cut in margarine until mixture resembles coarse crumbs; stir in fruit. Add combined milk and eggs, mixing just until moistened. Shape dough to form a ball.

Turn out onto lightly floured surface; knead gently 6 times. On lightly greased cookie sheet, pat out dough to form 8-inch circle. With sharp knife, score round into 12 wedges; sprinkle with combined sugar and cinnamon. Bake 20 to 25 minutes or until golden brown.

Yield: 12 triangular scones

Nutrition Facts

Nutrition (per serving): 232 calories, 79 calories from fat, 9g total fat, 26.8mg cholesterol, 279.8mg sodium, 79mg potassium, 34.7g carbohydrates, 1.5g fiber, 16.7g sugar, 4g protein.

George's Cherry Scones

2 cups all-purpose flour	1/3 cup butter or margarine
1/3 cup sugar	1 1/2 cups whipping cream, divided
1 Tbs. baking powder	3 oz. dried cherries
1/4 tsp. salt	2 Tbs. sugar

Procedure

Preheat oven to 375° F. Spray baking sheet with non-stick cooking spray or lightly grease.

Sift together first four ingredients; cut in butter with a pastry blender until crumbly. Add 1 ¼ cups whipping cream and cherries, stirring just until dry ingredients are moistened.

Turn dough out onto a lightly floured surface; knead 5 or 6 times. Pat or roll dough to ½-inch thickness; cut with a heart-shaped cutter, and place on a lightly greased baking sheet. Brush dough with remaining ¼ cup whipping cream; sprinkle evenly with 2 tablespoons sugar.

Bake at 375° for 12 to 15 minutes or until golden. Serve warm.

Yield: 12 scones

Nutrition Facts

Nutrition (per serving): 323 calories, 99 calories from fat, 11.3g total fat, 34mg cholesterol, 182.1mg sodium, 35.4mg potassium, 54.3g carbohydrates, 2.6g fiber, 7.7g sugar, 3.5g protein.

"Father, I cannot tell a lie; I cut the cherry tree" is a biographical myth about George Washington – and this really isn't his recipe.

Gingerbread Scones

1/4 cup	granulated sugar -- divided	1/8 tsp.	ground cloves
1 3/4 cup	all-purpose flour	1/3 cup	butter or margarine
3/4 cup	rolled oats	1/3 cup	skim milk
4 tsp.	baking powder	1/3 cup	dried currants
1 tsp.	ground ginger	2	egg whites, beaten
1/2 tsp.	ground cinnamon	2 Tbs.	molasses
1/4 tsp.	ground nutmeg		

Procedure

Preheat oven to 425 degrees F. Reserve 1 teaspoon of sugar. In a large bowl, combine remaining sugar with flour, oatmeal, baking powder, ginger, cinnamon, nutmeg, and cloves. Mix well. Cut in margarine until crumbly. In a small bowl, combine milk, currants, egg whites and molasses. Add to dry ingredients and mix just until moistened.

Turn dough onto lightly floured surface; knead gently 5 to 10 times. Roll or pat dough to 3/4-inch thickness. Cut with 2 1/2-inch heart-shaped or round biscuit cutter. Place on ungreased cookie sheet. Sprinkle tops with reserved teaspoon sugar. Bake for 9 to 12 minutes or until golden brown. Serve with Orange Breakfast Cream or orange marmalade.

Yield: 18 medium scones

Nutrition Facts

Nutrition (per serving): 121 calories, 36 calories from fat, 4.2g total fat, 10.6mg cholesterol, 131.5mg sodium, 92.3mg potassium, 18.5g carbohydrates, <1g fiber, 6g sugar, 3g protein.

Hazelnut Chocolate Scones

2	cup	all-purpose flour
1/3	cup	firmly packed dark brown sugar
1 1/2	tsp.	baking powder
1/2	tsp.	salt
6	Tbs.	unsalted butter, cold, cubed

1/2	cup	buttermilk
1		whole egg, large
1 1/2		tsp. vanilla extract
1	cup	semi-sweet chocolate chips
1/2	cup	Oregon hazelnuts, toasted and finely chopped

Procedure

Preheat oven to 400 degrees F. Lightly butter a 9-inch circle in the center of a baking sheet. In a large bowl, stir together the flour, brown sugar, baking powder, baking soda and salt. Cut the butter into the flour mixture until it resembles coarse crumbs. Stir together the buttermilk, egg and vanilla extract. Add the buttermilk mixture to the flour mixture and stir to combine. Stir in the chocolate chips and hazelnuts. The dough will be sticky.

Spread the dough into an 8-inch diameter circle in the center of the prepared baking sheet. Sprinkle with extra chopped hazelnuts, if desired. With a serrated knife, cut into eight wedges. Bake for about 18 minutes or until top is lightly browned. Remove to a wire rack and let cool for about 5 minutes. Transfer to a cutting board and cut into wedges.

Yield: 12 scones

Nutrition Facts

Nutrition (per serving): 236 calories, 97 calories from fat, 11.4g total fat, 33.3mg cholesterol, 179.6mg sodium, 76mg potassium, 31.7g carbohydrates, 1.5g fiber, 6.6g sugar, 3.8g protein.

Honey Oat Scones

1 1/2	cup	all-purpose flour	1/3 cup raisins
1	cup	quick cooking rolled oats	1/4 cup buttermilk nonfat -- plus
1	Tbs.	baking powder	additional 2 Tbs..
1/4 cup		honey	2 Tbs. skim milk
3	Tbs.	liquid egg substitute -	

Procedure

Preheat oven to 375 degrees F. Coat a baking sheet with cooking spray. Combine the flour, oats and baking powder; stir to mix well. Stir in the honey, egg substitute, raisins and buttermilk, adding just enough extra buttermilk to form a stiff dough.

Form the dough into a ball and turn onto a lightly floured surface. With floured hands, pat the dough into a 7-inch circle. Cut into 12 wedges and place on prepared baking sheet leaving 1/2-inch space between scones. Brush the tops lightly with skim milk. Bake for about 20 minutes or until lightly browned.

Yield: 12 triangular scones

Nutrition Facts

Nutrition (per serving): 125 calories, 7 calories from fat, <1g total fat, <1mg cholesterol, 134.4mg sodium, 104.9mg potassium, 26.6g carbohydrates, 1.3g fiber, 8.8g sugar, 3.6g protein.

Healthy, low fat scones taste great with Smart Balance or Earth Balance spreads.

Jennie Mae's Irish Scones

2 cups all-purpose flour

1 1/2 tsp. sugar (optional)

1/2 tsp. baking soda

1/4 tsp. salt

1/4 cup cold unsalted butter, cut into pieces

3/4 cup chilled buttermilk or sour milk (see note)

Procedure

Preheat oven to 400 degrees F. Sift the flour, sugar, baking soda and salt into a bowl. Rub in the butter until the mixture resembles coarse meal. Stir in the buttermilk all at once and mix with a spoon until all ingredients are moistened and a dough forms.

Turn out onto a lightly floured surface and knead about 4 or 5 times. Roll or pat the dough 1/2 to 1/4 inch thick and cut with a 2-inch cutter into rounds or diamonds approximately the same size, re-forming and re-cutting the scraps. Arrange the scones 2 inches apart on an ungreased baking sheet. Bake 13 to 16 minutes or until they are well risen and the tops are golden brown.

Yield: 12 scones

Nutrition Facts

Nutrition (per serving): 118 calories, 37 calories from fat, 4.2g total fat, 10.8mg cholesterol, 117.9mg sodium, 46.6mg potassium, 17.2g carbohydrates, <1g fiber, 1.3g sugar, 2.7g protein.

Note: To sour 3/4 c. of milk, combine 1 tsp. fresh lemon juice or vinegar with the milk and let stand for 10 to 15 minutes or until thickened and curdled.

King's Mountain Apple Scones

1 1/4   cup   all-purpose flour

4   Tbs. brown sugar, divided

1/4 tsp. salt

1/4 tsp. baking soda

1   tsp. baking powder

1/4 cup   butter or margarine

1   cup   peeled apples, chopped

1/4 cup   light sour cream

1   whole egg, beaten

1/3 cup   chopped pecans

Topping

1   Tbs. light sour cream

1/4 tsp. cinnamon

Procedure

Preheat oven to 400 degrees F. Lightly coat a baking sheet with non-stick cooking spray. In large mixing bowl, combine flour, 3 tablespoons brown sugar, salt, soda and baking powder. Cut in margarine until mixture resembles coarse crumbs. Add apples, the 1/4-cup sour cream, egg and pecans, mixing until combined. On floured surface, lightly knead.

Place on prepared cookie sheet. With floured hands, press into 8-inch circle. Cut circle into 8 wedges with floured sharp knife. Do not separate wedges. Brush top of dough with tablespoon sour cream and sprinkle with mixture of tablespoon sugar and cinnamon. Bake about 15 minutes or until golden brown.

Yield: 8 scones

Nutrition Facts

Nutrition (per serving): 217 calories, 100 calories from fat, 11.5g total fat, 47.2mg cholesterol, 196.7mg sodium, 119.4mg potassium, 25.4g carbohydrates, 1.2g fiber, 8.3g sugar, 3.9g protein.

Lavender Orange Scones

2	cups unbleached all-purpose flour	5	Tbs.	orange zest, grated
1/2	tsp. salt	2	Tbs.	lavender blossoms, finely chopped
1	Tbs. baking powder			
1	Tbs. sugar	1 1/4	cup	sour cream

Procedure

Preheat the oven to 400 degrees F. Lightly oil a large cookie sheet. Stir together the flour, salt, baking powder, sugar, orange zest, and lavender in a large bowl. Gradually stir in enough sour cream to form a sticky dough.

Turn the dough onto a floured board. Knead by gently folding the dough in half a dozen times or so until it no longer sticks to the board. Roll or press to 1/2 inch thickness.

Cut into 2-inch rounds. Place on the prepared sheet, and bake until lightly browned, about 12 minutes.

Yield: 12 scones

Nutrition Facts

Nutrition (per serving): 117 calories, 28 calories from fat, 3.2g total fat, 9.8mg cholesterol, 229.6mg sodium, 60.4mg potassium, 19g carbohydrates, <1g fiber, 1.2g sugar, 2.9g protein.

Orange zest gives an appealing lift to the lavender petals in Lavender Orange Scones.

Lavender Walnut Scones

2 cups all-purpose flour
1 Tbs. baking powder
1/4 tsp. baking soda
1/2 tsp. salt
1/2 cup sugar
2 Tbs. lavender blossoms
2 Tbs. margarine
1 cup nonfat buttermilk

1 Tbs. vanilla nut extract

Topping

3 Tbs. walnuts, finely chopped
2 Tbs. sugar

Procedure

Preheat oven to 400 degrees F. Lightly coat a baking sheet with cooking spray. Sift together first 5 ingredients into a medium mixing bowl. Cut in margarine with a pastry blender until mixture resembles coarse meal. Add buttermilk and vanilla extract, stirring with a fork until dry ingredients are moistened.

Drop dough by 4 oz. scoop or large spoon, 2 inches apart onto baking sheet. Sprinkle scones evenly with walnuts and remaining sugar. Bake for 15 to 17 minutes or until golden brown.

Yield: 12 drop scones

Nutrition Facts

Nutrition (per serving): 143 calories, 30 calories from fat, 3.4g total fat, 2.9mg cholesterol, 191.3mg sodium, 64.6mg potassium, 25.1g carbohydrates, <1g fiber, 8.7g sugar, 3.3g protein.

Lemon Blueberry Scones

2	cup	all-purpose flour	5	Tbs.	butter
3	Tbs.	sugar	2/3	cup	heavy cream, divided
3	tsp.	baking powder	1/2	cup	blueberries
1/4	tsp.	salt	1	each	zest of one lemon
1/2	tsp.	freshly grated nutmeg	1	whole	egg, beaten

Procedure

Preheat oven to 425 degrees F. Line a pan with parchment paper. Sift dry ingredients into a large bowl. Cut the butter into the flour mixture until it resembles coarse breadcrumbs. Add the blueberries and lemon zest coating with the flour mixture. Reserve one tablespoon cream. Make a well into the ingredients and add the remaining cream. Stir with your hands until blended. Knead lightly and do not over mix.

Put dough onto a floured board and shape into a circle about 1" thick. Move to a parchment lined pan cut into 8 wedges and coat top lightly with egg wash of one tablespoon cream and one beaten egg. Bake 16-18 minutes or until golden brown.

Yield: 8 scones.

Nutrition Facts

Nutrition (per serving): 280 calories, 137 calories from fat, 15.6g total fat, 72.7mg cholesterol, 273.6mg sodium, 67.9mg potassium, 31.2g carbohydrates, 1.2g fiber, 5.9g sugar, 4.6g protein.

Lemon Ginger Scones

2	cups	all-purpose flour
1/4	cup	granulated sugar
1	tsp.	baking soda
1	tsp.	cream of tartar
1/4	cup	candied ginger, finely chopped
2	tsp.	grated lemon zest
1	cup	low fat buttermilk

1	Tbs.	Canola oil

Topping

1	large egg, beaten	
1	Tbs.	water
1	Tbs.	sugar

Procedure

Preheat oven to 350° F. Lightly coat a baking sheet with non-stick cooking spray. In a medium bowl, mix together flour, 1/4-cup sugar, baking soda and cream of tartar. Stir in the candied ginger and lemon zest. In a small bowl, combine the buttermilk and oil. Add to the dry ingredients, stirring just until blended.

Turn the slightly sticky dough out onto a lightly floured work surface and pat to 1/2-inch thickness. Using a floured, 4-inch round cutter, cut out the dough. Cut each circle in half to make semi-circles or crescents. Reroll and cut the scraps, handling the dough as little as possible. Place scones onto the prepared baking sheet. In a small bowl, lightly beat the egg with the water. Brush the tops of the scones with the egg glaze. Lightly sprinkle the scones with sugar. Bake 15 to 20 minutes or until tops are golden brown.

Yield: 16 scones

Nutrition Facts

Nutrition (per serving): 100 calories, 13 calories from fat, 1.5g total fat, 13.8mg cholesterol, 99.6mg sodium, 75.4mg potassium, 19.1g carbohydrates, <1g fiber, 4.7g sugar, 2.5g protein.

Liberty Bell Scones

2 cups self-rising flour
2 Tbs. sugar
1 tsp. poppy seeds
2 tsp. lemon rind, grated
1/3 cup butter
1/2 cup buttermilk

1 whole egg, lightly beaten
1 Tbs. milk

GLAZE

1 1/2 Tbs. lemon juice
1 cup powdered sugar

Procedure

Preheat oven to 425 degrees F. Lightly grease a baking sheet. Sift together flour and sugar; add poppy seeds and grated lemon rind; cut in butter until crumbly. Add buttermilk and egg; stir until moistened. Turn dough onto lightly floured surface and knead 5 to 6 times. Divide dough in half; roll each portion into a 6-inch circle. Cut each circle into 8 wedges and place 1-inch apart on prepared baking sheet. Bake for 12 to 15 minutes or until golden brown.

GLAZE

Combine fresh lemon juice with powdered sugar and drizzle over warm scones.

Yield: 8 wedges

Nutrition Facts

Nutrition (per serving): 211 calories, 78 calories from fat, 8.9g total fat, 47.5mg cholesterol, 423.6mg sodium, 83mg potassium, 28g carbohydrates, <1g fiber, 4.6g sugar, 4.6g protein.

Loyal Oat Scones

4	cups all-purpose flour		4	whole large eggs, beaten
1	cup whole-wheat flour		1	whole large egg, beaten with one Tbs. water
1	cup quick-cooking oats			
2	Tbs. baking powder			**GLAZE**
2	Tbs. granulated sugar		1 1/4	cup confectioners' sugar
2	tsp. salt		1/2	cup pure maple syrup
1	cup cold unsalted butter		1	tsp. pure vanilla extract
1/2	cup cold buttermilk			
1/2	cup pure maple syrup			

Procedure

Preheat oven to 400° F. Line a baking sheet with parchment paper. In a mixing bowl, combine 3 ½ cups all-purpose flour, whole wheat flour, oats, baking powder, sugar, and salt. Blend in the butter until mixture resembles cornmeal. In a medium bowl, combine buttermilk, maple syrup, and 4 eggs; stir well. Add egg mixture to flour mixture. Mix until well blended.

Place dough on a floured surface. Roll dough to a ¾" thickness with a floured rolling pin. Cut into 3-inch rounds with a plain or fluted cutter and place on the prepared baking sheet. Brush tops with egg wash. Bake 20 to 25 minutes. Cool on wire rack.

Glaze: Combine confectioners' sugar, maple syrup, and vanilla. Drizzle each cooled scone with 1 tablespoon glaze.

Yield: 28 scones

Nutrition Facts
Nutrition (per serving): 192 calories, 70 calories from fat, 7.9g total fat, 55.4mg cholesterol, 290.1mg sodium, 76.1mg potassium, 26.6g carbohydrates, <1g fiber, 8.3g sugar, 3.9g protein.

Maple Pecan Scones

3/4 cup pecans, toasted	3/4 cup whipping cream
2 1/4 cups all-purpose flour	**Maple Butter:**
1 tsp. baking powder	1/3 cup butter -- softened
1/4 tsp. baking soda	1/4 cup maple syrup
1/4 tsp. salt	1/4 tsp. ground cinnamon
1/3 cup maple syrup	

Procedure

Preheat oven to 425° F. Lightly grease a baking sheet. In a food processor bowl, grind 1/3 cup pecans. Chop remaining pecans. Combine the ground pecans, the chopped pecans, flour, baking powder, baking soda, and salt. Add the syrup and whipping cream, stirring until the dry ingredients are moistened.

Turn the dough out onto a lightly floured surface and knead 4 to 5 times. Pat the dough out into two 6-inch rounds on the baking sheet. Using a sharp knife, make 8 shallow cuts in the dough forming wedges. Bake 10 to 12 minutes or until lightly browned.

Maple Whipped Butter:

Beat the butter until fluffy; mix in the syrup and cinnamon.

Yield: 16 wedge scones

Nutrition Facts

Nutrition (per serving): 203 calories, 102 calories from fat, 11.8g total fat, 25.4mg cholesterol, 92.7mg sodium, 73.5mg potassium, 22.4g carbohydrates, <1g fiber, 7.3g sugar, 2.6g protein.

Maple Scones are delicious served with cinnamon butter. For a different tweak, add 1/2 cup finely chopped black walnuts to the dough before baking.

Mornin' Glory Scones

2 cups all-purpose flour	1 cup currants
1 Tbs. baking powder	2 egg yolks, beaten
1/2 tsp. salt	1 whole egg
1/2 cup granulated sugar	4 Tbs. milk
1/2 cup butter -- cut in pieces	

Procedure

Preheat oven to 375 degrees F. Lightly grease baking sheet. Sift together the flour, baking powder, salt and granulated sugar in large bowl. Add butter and mix with electric mixer on low speed (or by hand with pastry blender) until mixture resembles coarse cornmeal. Stir in currants. In small bowl, beat egg yolks, 1 egg and milk until blended; pour over flour mixture. Mix lightly until mixture holds together; form into ball.

Roll out dough to 3/4 -inch thickness. Use 2-1/2-inch round biscuit cutter to make at least 9 scones (reroll scraps until all dough is used). Place scones on greased baking sheet. Beat remaining egg; brush over scones. Bake 14 to 18 minutes or until brown. Cool on rack for at least 15 minutes before serving.

Yield: 12 scones

Nutrition Facts

Nutrition (per serving): 228 calories, 81 calories from fat, 9.2g total fat, 73.3mg cholesterol, 230.5mg sodium, 148.3mg potassium, 33.8g carbohydrates, 1.4g fiber, 16.8g sugar, 3.9g protein.

Excellent with Crème Chantilly and Peach Marmalade along with a pot of Pure Ceylon Tea.

Oatmeal Breakfast Scones

1	cup	all-purpose flour
1	cup	rolled oats
1/2	tsp.	baking soda
1/2	tsp.	salt

1	tsp.	cream of tartar
1	Tbs.	sugar
1/4	cup	shortening
1/2	cup	milk

Procedure

Preheat oven to 425 degrees F. Mix together flour, oats, baking soda, salt, cream of tartar, and sugar. Add the shortening and milk, and mix with fork into a soft dough. Roll out on a floured surface to 1/2" thickness. Cut into triangles. Place on greased baking sheet and bake for 15 minutes or until lightly browned.

Yield: 12 scones

Nutrition Facts

Nutrition (per serving): 138 calories, 50 calories from fat, 5.7g total fat, <1mg cholesterol, 154.1mg sodium, 123.5mg potassium, 18.2g carbohydrates, 1.7g fiber, 1.6g sugar, 3.6g protein.

Orange Date Scones

1 3/4	cup	flour	1	whole egg, beaten
1/2 cup	sugar		2	Tbs. milk
3/4 tsp.	baking powder		1	tsp. orange zest, grated
1/2 tsp.	salt		1/2	tsp. vanilla extract
1/4 tsp.	baking soda		2/3	cup chopped dates
1/2 cup	butter			

Procedure

Preheat oven to 350°F. Combine all dry ingredients. Cut in butter and add chopped dates. Combine all liquids and add to dry ingredients. Gently shape dough into a ball; place on floured board and pat into a large circle about 1/2" thick.

Cut into wedges, place on baking sheet and bake at 350 degrees F. for about 15 to 20 minutes or until golden brown.

Yield: 8 wedges

Nutrition Facts

Nutrition (per serving): 304 calories, 110 calories from fat, 12.5g total fat, 57.3mg cholesterol, 243.1mg sodium, 145.4mg potassium, 44.9g carbohydrates, 2g fiber, 22.2g sugar, 4.2g protein.

Orange Pecan Scones

2	cups	self-rising flour	1/4	cup	fresh orange juice
1/2	cup	sugar	1/2	cup	pecans, finely chopped
2	tsp.	grated orange rind	1	tsp.	vanilla extract
1/3	cup	butter	1	tsp.	orange extract
1/2	cup	buttermilk			Sugar, additional for sprinkling tops

Procedure

Preheat oven to 425 degrees F. Combine first 3 ingredients. Cut butter into flour mixture with a pastry blender until crumbly; add buttermilk and next four ingredients, stirring just until dry ingredients are moistened. Turn dough out onto a lightly floured surface; knead 3 or 4 times.

Divide dough in half; pat each portion into a 7-inch circle, and place on a lightly greased baking sheet. Cut each circle into 8 wedges; sprinkle evenly with sugar. Bake for 12 to 14 minutes or until golden brown.

Yield: 16 scones

Nutrition Facts

Nutrition (per serving): 147 calories, 56 calories from fat, 6.5g total fat, 10.5mg cholesterol, 207.1mg sodium, 55.2mg potassium, 20g carbohydrates, <1g fiber, 8g sugar, 2.2g protein.

Patriotic Pear Scones

1	cup	all-purpose flour, unbleached	3/4	cup	pears -- finely chopped
3/4	cup	whole wheat flour	1/3	cup	currants or raisins
1	Tbs.	baking powder	2	Tbs.	skim milk -- to 3 Tbs.
3	Tbs.	maple syrup			additional skim milk
3	Tbs.	liquid egg substitute			

Procedure

Preheat oven to 375 degrees F. Coat a baking sheet with non-stick cooking spray. Combine the flours and baking powder and stir to mix well. Stir in the syrup, egg substitute, pears, currants, and just enough of the milk to form a stiff dough. Form the dough into a ball and turn onto a lightly floured surface.

With floured hands, pat the dough into a 7-inch circle. Place the dough on the baking sheet and use a sharp knife to cut it into 12 wedges. Pull the wedges out slightly to leave a 1/2-inch space between them. Brush the tops lightly with skim milk. Bake for about 20 minutes or until lightly browned.

Yield: 12 wedges

Nutrition Facts

Nutrition (per serving): 112 calories, 7 calories from fat, <1g total fat, 1.9mg cholesterol, 139.6mg sodium, 125.4mg potassium, 23.2g carbohydrates, 1.1g fiber, 7.9g sugar, 3.3g protein.

Peace Treaty Potato Scones

2 cups all-purpose flour	1 cup mashed potatoes
1 Tbs. baking powder	1/3 cup milk
1 tsp. salt	1 whole egg
3 Tbs. cold butter	

Procedure

Preheat oven to 400° F. In a bowl, combine the flour, baking powder and salt. Cut in butter until mixture resembles coarse crumbs. Combine potatoes, milk and egg; stir into the crumb mixture until a soft dough forms. Turn onto a floured surface; knead gently 10-12 minutes or until no longer sticky. Roll dough into a circle about 3/4 inch thick. With biscuit cutter, cut dough. Separate rounds and place on an ungreased baking sheet. Bake for 15-18 minutes or until golden brown.

Yield: 12 scones

Nutrition Facts

Nutrition (per serving): 126 calories, 33 calories from fat, 3.7g total fat, 26.2mg cholesterol, 378mg sodium, 91mg potassium, 19.6g carbohydrates, <1g fiber, <1g sugar, 3.3g protein.

Potato Tomato Herb Scones

1 1/2 cups self-rising flour

1/2   cup mashed potatoes

1/4   tsp. baking soda

2   Tbs. grated Parmesan

2   whole eggs, lightly beaten

2   Tbs. chopped sun-dried tomatoes

2   Tbs. minced rosemary

2   Tbs. minced thyme

1   Tbs. grated Parmesan cheese, extra

        Extra 1/4 cup milk

Procedure

Preheat oven to 425° F. Brush bottom of scone baking tray with melted butter or oil. Coat with flour; shake off excess. Combine all ingredients except for extra Parmesan and extra milk in a food processor bowl. Using pulse action, process for 15 seconds or until the mixture comes together. Turn mixture onto a floured surface. Knead lightly for about 2 minutes or until smooth. Pat dough out to 1/2" thickness. Cut into rounds with a 2" biscuit cutter dipped in flour.

Place scones close together in tray. Brush tops with extra milk, sprinkle with the extra Parmesan.

Bake for 10 to 15 minutes or until scones are well risen and golden. Serve hot with butter.

Yield: 18 scones

Nutrition Facts

Nutrition (per serving): 56 calories, 9 calories from fat, 1g total fat, 24.6mg cholesterol, 197.2mg sodium, 57.9mg potassium, 9.2g carbohydrates, <1g fiber, <1g sugar, 2.3g protein.

Pumpkin Curry and Ginger Scones

3	cups	all-purpose flour		
1	Tbs.	baking powder		
1/2	tsp.	baking soda		
3/4	tsp.	salt		
1/2	cup	chopped candied ginger		
1/2	tsp.	curry powder		

1/4 tsp. turmeric
5 Tbs. granulated sugar
1/2 cup butter, cold and cut into small chunks
1/2 cup cooked, pureed pumpkin or squash
1 cup buttermilk, plain yogurt or sour cream

Procedure

Preheat oven to 425°F. Lightly grease a baking sheet. In a medium-sized mixing bowl, mix together the flour, baking powder, baking soda, salt, ginger, curry, turmeric and sugar. Cut in the butter with a pastry blender until the mixture resembles coarse crumbs.

In a separate bowl, beat together the pumpkin or squash and buttermilk, yogurt or sour cream until smooth. Add the pumpkin mixture to the dry ingredients, stirring until just combined.

Turn the dough out onto a lightly floured work surface and pat or roll it into a 10-inch square about 1/2 to 3/4-inch thick. Cut the large square into 2-inch squares and transfer them to the baking sheet leaving about an inch between scones.

Bake 20 minutes or until golden brown.

Yield: 24 scones

Nutrition Facts

Nutrition (per serving): 119 calories, 36 calories from fat, 4.1g total fat, 10.6mg cholesterol, 183.7mg sodium, 45.2mg potassium, 18.7g carbohydrates, <1g fiber, 3.2g sugar, 2.1g protein.

Pumpkin Bumpkin Scones

6	Tbs. butter, cold and cubed	4	tsp.	baking powder
1	cup sugar	1/2	tsp.	cinnamon
1	whole egg, beaten	1/2	tsp.	salt
1	Tbs. milk	1/2	cup	raisins
2	cups mashed pumpkin	1		egg white, beaten
3	cups all-purpose flour			

Procedure

Preheat oven to 425°F. Lightly grease a baking sheet.

Cream margarine and sugar; add beaten egg, milk, and mashed pumpkin; set aside. In a separate bowl, sift together flour, baking powder, cinnamon, and salt. Add to creamed mixture and stir just until moistened. Stir in raisins. Place dough on floured board and knead 5 or 6 times. Roll to 1/2-inch thickness. With sharp knife, cut into 4-inch triangles.

Place on greased baking sheet. Brush tops with beaten egg white and bake for 20 minutes or until edges are lightly browned.

Yield: 24 scones

Nutrition Facts

Nutrition (per serving): 136 calories, 29 calories from fat, 3.3g total fat, 12mg cholesterol, 216.9mg sodium, 92.4mg potassium, 25g carbohydrates, 1.2g fiber, 10.5g sugar, 2.4g protein.

Queen Mother Scones

2	cups all-purpose flour		1/4 cup	butter, cold, cubed
3	tsp. baking powder		3	whole eggs, beaten
1/2 tsp.	salt		1/3 cup	half-and-half cream
2	Tbs. sugar		2	Tbs. milk
1	cup currants			

Procedure

Preheat oven to 350 degrees F. Sift together dry ingredients including currants*. Blend in butter until mixture resembles coarse meal. Whisk together 2 eggs, saving one for later, and cream in a separate bowl. Combine with flour mixture. Gently form a soft dough. Cover dough with plastic wrap and let rest in the refrigerator for 30 minutes or more. Dust dough lightly with flour and roll to 1" thickness. Cut 2-inch rounds and place on baking sheet. Mix remaining egg with 2 tablespoons milk and brush scones with egg mixture. Bake for approximately 20 to 25 minutes or until golden brown.

VARIATION:

To make Ginger Scones, add finely chopped candied ginger instead of currants. Serve with a lemon glaze.

*Dust the currants in flour before adding them to mixture so they won't drop to the bottom when baking.

Yield: 24 2-inch scones

Nutrition Facts

Nutrition (per serving): 90 calories, 27 calories from fat, 3.1g total fat, 32.9mg cholesterol, 121mg sodium, 80mg potassium, 13.9g carbohydrates, <1g fiber, 5.2g sugar, 2.3g protein.

Recipe contributed by: Margaret Nevills – Red Hat Society

Rice Flour Scones

2	cups rice flour	1 1/2	tsp.	egg white replacement
2	tsp. baking powder	1/3 cup	butter, cold, cubed	
1/4 cup	white sugar	1/2 cup	plus 3 Tbs. soy milk	
1	tsp. xanthum gum*	3/4 cup	raisins or currants	
1	tsp. salt			

Procedure

Preheat oven to 400 degrees F. Sift all dry ingredients together. Cut margarine into flour mixture until no large lumps remain (coarse cornmeal). Make a well in the dry ingredients and add the vanilla soymilk. Add a little more flour if necessary. If using raisins or currants, add them now. The dough will be a little stiff.

On a rice-floured surface, roll dough to ½" thick. Dough is somewhat fragile and will crack a little around the edges – be careful when rolling. Cut with a 2" biscuit cutter and place on baking sheet. Bake for about 15 minutes or until slightly brown. Rice Flour Scones remain white after baking and do not turn golden brown. They are very tender and we sometimes call them "Wedding Scones".

*Find xanthum gum in the "health food" section at the market.

Yield: 12 rice scones

Nutrition Facts

Nutrition (per serving): 217 calories, 76 calories from fat, 8.6g total fat, 8.3mg cholesterol, 370mg sodium, 171.8mg potassium, 33.3g carbohydrates, 1.7g fiber, 10.3g sugar, 2.8g protein.

*So tender! And gluten free! Beautiful for a
"White Tea" or Bridal Shower.*

Rose Petal Drop Scones

2 1/4	cup	all-purpose flour
2	tsp.	sugar
3/4	tsp.	salt
2	tsp.	baking powder
1/2	tsp.	baking soda
1/2	tsp.	cinnamon
4	Tbs.	unsalted butter
1/3	cup	unsalted pistachio nuts, ground

1	cup	heavy cream
1	Tbs.	rose water
2	Tbs.	edible rose petals, finely shredded

Icing

1	cup	powdered sugar
1	Tbs.	rose jelly, plum jelly or red currant jelly
2	tsp.	rose water, plus extra if needed

Procedure

Preheat oven to 425° F. Combine the flour, sugar, salt, baking powder, baking soda, and cinnamon. Cut in the butter to resemble coarse crumbs. Stir in the pistachios. In a separate bowl, combine the cream and the rose water. Stir in rose petals. Add the cream-rose mixture to the dry ingredients, stirring until a soft dough forms. Drop by teaspoonsful onto an ungreased cookie sheet. Bake for 10-12 minutes or until golden brown.

Prepare the icing:

Whisk together the powdered sugar, rose water, and the plum jelly. Drizzle over scones. Garnish with fresh roses.

Yield: 24 small scones

Nutrition Facts

Nutrition (per serving): 107 calories, 57 calories from fat, 6.5g total fat, 18.7mg cholesterol, 148.3mg sodium, 41.1mg potassium, 10.6g carbohydrates, <1g fiber, <1g sugar, 1.8g protein.

Rosemary Olive Scones

1/3 cup	half and half or milk	2 tsp.	baking powder
2	whole eggs, beaten	1/2 tsp.	crushed dried rosemary
1/3 cup	finely chopped green onion	1/4 tsp.	crushed dried sage
1/4 cup	ripe olives, chopped	3/4 tsp.	black pepper
1 1/2 cup	all-purpose flour	1/2 tsp.	salt, optional
1 cup	uncooked rolled oats	1/2 cup	butter, chilled
1 Tbs.	sugar		

Procedure

Heat oven to 450° F. Grease a cookie sheet. Combine and set aside half-and-half, eggs, onion, and olives. In a large bowl, combine and mix well: flour, oats, sugar, baking powder, rosemary, sage, pepper, and salt. With a pastry blender, or 2 knives, cut butter into the dry mixture. Stop when the mixture resembles coarse crumbs. Add liquid ingredients. Mix just until dry ingredients are moistened. Do not over mix.

Turn out onto lightly floured surface. Knead 8 or 10 times. Pat dough into an 8-inch circle, about 3/4 inch thick. Cut into 8 wedges. Place wedges on prepared cookie sheet. Bake for 18 to 20 minutes, or until light golden brown. Serve warm.

Yield: Cut into 8 wedges

Nutrition Facts

Nutrition (per serving): 264 calories, 125 calories from fat, 14.3g total fat, 84.2mg cholesterol, 328.2mg sodium, 109.1mg potassium, 28.2g carbohydrates, 1.9g fiber, 2.7g sugar, 6.2g protein.

Rosy Raisin Scones

3 1/2	cups flour	1	large egg, beaten
1/2 cup	sugar	1/2 cup	milk
1/8 tsp.	salt	1/4 cup	rose syrup
1 Tbs.	baking powder	1/2 cup	raisins
3/4 cup	butter	1	large egg, beaten

Procedure

Preheat oven to 400°F. Sift together the flour, sugar, salt and baking powder. Using a pastry blender, cut the butter into the flour mixture until crumbly. Add sugar and raisins.

Make well in center of the mixture; add one egg, rose syrup and small amount of milk. If mixture appears to be too dry, add more milk. Blend to a smooth dough. Roll out on floured board to 1/2 inch thick. Use 2-inch cutter with fluted edge. Place on lightly greased baking sheet, brush with beaten egg.

Bake in 400-degree F oven for 10-15 minutes or until golden brown.

Yield: 3 dozen scones

Nutrition Facts

Nutrition (per serving): 108 calories, 38 calories from fat, 4.3g total fat, 22.2mg cholesterol, 57.8mg sodium, 40.3mg potassium, 16g carbohydrates, <1g fiber, 6.2g sugar, 1.8g protein.

The delicate scent of rose petals is heavenly. Rose syrup is available at most Middle Eastern markets or you can make your own by adding a tablespoon of rose water to one cup of simple syrup.

Saratoga Oat Cakes

2 cups self-rising flour
1/2 cup sugar
1/2 tsp. cinnamon
1/2 tsp. mace

3 cups uncooked oatmeal
1/2 cup walnuts, finely chopped
1/4 cup butter, cold
1 cup boiling water, divided

Procedure

Preheat oven to 350 degrees F. Lightly grease a cookie sheet. Sift together the flour, sugar and spices. Cut in butter until mixture resembles coarse crumbs. Add nuts. Gradually add boiling water, 2 tablespoons at a time, until mixture clings together. Turn out onto a lightly floured surface and gently roll dough to about 1/4-inch thickness. Cut with a 2-inch cookie cutter. Transfer to baking sheet. Bake for about 12 to 15 minutes or until lightly browned.

Yield: 2 dozen

Nutrition Facts

Nutrition (per serving): 103 calories, 32 calories from fat, 3.8g total fat, 5.1mg cholesterol, 133mg sodium, 45.3mg potassium, 16g carbohydrates, 1.1g fiber, 4.3g sugar, 2g protein.

Scottish Tea Scones

1-1/4	cups rolled oats put through food chopper		1-1/2	cups bread flour
2	Tbs. vegetable oil		1	Tbs. cornstarch
2/3 cup	scalded milk		3	tsp. baking powder
2	Tbs. light corn syrup		3/4 tsp.	salt

Procedure

Put the oatmeal in a small mixing bowl; add the vegetable oil, corn syrup and hot milk. Let cool. Sift the remaining ingredients and add to the cooled milk mixture. Mix, turn onto a floured board and divide into two portions.

Roll each into a round cake, one-half inch thick, cut into four triangles, bake on an oiled, hot griddle, turning only once. Allow about fifteen minutes for the cooking. Serve with butter, plain or with any marmalade or jelly.

Yield: 8

Nutrition Facts

Nutrition (per serving): 202 calories, 45 calories from fat, 5.1g total fat, 1.6mg cholesterol, 416.4mg sodium, 101.1mg potassium, 33.4g carbohydrates, 1.9g fiber, 5.3g sugar, 5.8g protein.

Soy Flour Scones

1/2 cup soy bean flour	1 tsp. salt
4 Tbs. sorghum flour	1 1/2 tsp. egg replacement
2/3 cup cornstarch	1/3 cup butter, cold, diced
2/3 cup tapioca flour	1/2 cup plus 3 Tbs. vanilla soy beverage
2 tsp. baking powder	**Optional:**
1/4 cup white sugar	3/4 cup raisins or currants
1 tsp. xanthum gum	

Procedure

Preheat oven to 400 degrees F. Blend all dry ingredients together. Cut margarine into flour until mixture resembles coarse cornmeal. Add the vanilla soy beverage and mix until well blended. Dough will be slightly stiff. If adding dried fruit, do so now. On a bean-floured surface, roll dough to ½-inch thickness. Dough will crack around the edges. Take care; it is tender. Cut with a 2" biscuit cutter and carefully transfer to a baking sheet. Bake for about 15 minutes or until slightly brown.

Yield: 10 scones

Nutrition Facts

Nutrition (per serving): 227 calories, 58 calories from fat, 6.7g total fat, 16.3mg cholesterol, 342mg sodium, 145.9mg potassium, 41.1g carbohydrates, 1.8g fiber, 12.8g sugar, 2.3g protein.

Scones with protein and without gluten!

Spicy Fruit Oat Scones

1 1/4	cup	all-purpose flour or whole wheat flour	1/2 cup	uncooked oatmeal

1 1/4   cup   all-purpose flour or whole
             wheat flour

3   Tbs. sugar

2 1/2   tsp. baking powder

3/4 tsp. ground cinnamon

1/2 tsp. ground mace

1/8 tsp. ground cloves

1/4 tsp. salt

1/2 cup   uncooked oatmeal

1/3 cup   butter, cold, cubed

1   large egg, beaten

1/2 cup   currants or dates

4 to 6   Tbs. half-and-half cream

1   large egg, beaten

Procedure

Heat oven to 400° F. Sift dry ingredients into medium bowl, stir in oatmeal. Cut butter into oatmeal mix until mixture looks like crumbs. Stir in one egg, dried fruit, and just enough half-and-half so dough leaves the side of the bowl.

Turn dough onto lightly flour surface. Knead lightly; pat to 1/2-inch thick; cut with floured biscuit cutter. Place on ungreased baking sheet. Brush dough with remaining beaten egg.

Bake 10 to 12 minutes or until golden brown. *Immediately* remove from cookie sheet to wire rack. Serve plain or seasonally decorated.

Yield: 18 scones

Nutrition Facts

Nutrition (per serving): 106 calories, 41 calories from fat, 4.6g total fat, 33.8mg cholesterol, 110.5mg sodium, 65.3mg potassium, 14.3g carbohydrates, <1g fiber, 4.9g sugar, 2.2g protein.

For seasonal appeal, use dried blueberries, cherries, or cranberries in place of the raisins.

St. Augustine Scones

1	package active dry yeast	4	cups all-purpose flour
1	Tbs. milk, warmed	5	Tbs. butter
1	tsp. sugar	1	tsp. salt
1	cup whole milk	1/2 cup	sugar
3	whole large eggs, beaten		

Procedure

Dissolve yeast in tablespoon warm milk with 1 teaspoon of sugar. Scald milk; add butter, sugar and salt. Cool to lukewarm and add to yeast. Add beaten eggs, then add 2 cups flour and beat thoroughly. Add remainder of flour gradually.

Cover and place in refrigerator overnight. Four hours before baking, remove from refrigerator.

Preheat oven to 350°F. Divide dough into 4 parts and roll each to 1/4 inch thick. Brush with melted butter. Cut into 4 wedge shapes and roll each strip beginning at wide end and rolling toward point. Form into crescent shape. Place on greased baking sheet, cover and let rise 4 hours.

Bake at **350° F** for 20 minutes or until golden brown.

Yield: 16 crescent scones

Nutrition Facts

Nutrition (per serving): 194 calories, 46 calories from fat, 5.2g total fat, 50.5mg cholesterol, 166.4mg sodium, 80.3mg potassium, 31.4g carbohydrates, <1g fiber, 7.5g sugar, 5.2g protein.

Stilton Scones

8	oz.	self-rising flour	4	oz.	Stilton blue cheese
1/4	tsp.	cayenne pepper	5	oz.	milk
1/2	tsp.	dry mustard	1		whole beaten egg
2	oz.	butter			

Procedure

Preheat oven to 450° F. Sieve together the flour, salt, pepper and mustard. Rub in the butter and cheese and enough milk to make not too wet dough. On a floured board, roll out to 1/2" thick, cut into rounds and lightly brush with beaten egg and milk.

On a greased and floured baking sheet, bake for 10 minutes or until golden brown. Serve warm with butter.

Yield: Serves 4

Nutrition Facts

Nutrition (per serving): 351 calories, 194 calories from fat, 22g total fat, 89.7mg cholesterol, 952.7mg sodium, 194.4mg potassium, 25.9g carbohydrates, <1g fiber, 2.3g sugar, 12.2g protein.

Recipe contributed by: Joyce Sherwood, Melton Mowbray, Leicestershire, UK. Reprinted with permission of Stilton Cheese.

Sun Dried Cranberry Scones

3/4 cup   butter

1/2 cup   sugar, plus extra

5   large whole eggs

1   tsp.   pure vanilla extract

2   cups all-purpose flour

1   tsp.   baking powder

1   cup   milk

1/2 cup   dried cranberries or raisins,
soaked in 1/2 cup warm water
for 1/2 hour, then drained

1   large egg, mixed with 1 Tbs. water

Procedure

Preheat oven to 375° F. Line a baking sheet with parchment paper coated with egg wash.

Cream together the butter and sugar. Mix in eggs, one at a time. Add vanilla. Sift flour and baking powder together. Blend into butter mixture. Add milk and knead gently. Do not overwork dough. Add drained cranberries or raisins.

Let dough rest for 10-15 minutes. Roll dough to about 1/2-inch thick. Using a 2-inch cutter, cut dough into scones. Placed scones on prepared baking sheet. Bake for 15-20 minutes or until lightly browned.

Yield: 24 scones

Nutrition Facts

Nutrition (per serving): 171 calories, 66 calories from fat, 7.5g total fat, 68.9mg cholesterol, 43.4mg sodium, 51mg potassium, 22.9g carbohydrates, 1.1g fiber, 4.8g sugar, 3g protein.

Suffolk Place Scones

4 cups all-purpose flour	7 oz. milk
1 Tbs. baking powder	**Egg wash:**
1/2 cup butter	1 large egg, beaten
1 cup sugar	2 Tbs. water
3 large eggs, lightly beaten	

Procedure

Preheat oven to 400° F. Into a large bowl, sift the flour, baking powder and sugar together. With a pastry blender, cut the butter into the mixture until it resembles coarse meal. Add the eggs and milk and mix with a fork until a soft pliable dough forms.

On a lightly floured surface roll out the dough to a 1/2" thickness. Cut out shapes with a biscuit cutter. Brush the tops with an egg wash.

Heat an ungreased baking sheet in the oven until warm, place the scones on the sheet, and bake near the top of the oven until they are a light golden brown about 10-15 minutes.

Yield: 28 scones

Nutrition Facts

Nutrition (per serving): 136 calories, 38 calories from fat, 4.3g total fat, 39.5mg cholesterol, 66.2mg sodium, 41.3mg potassium, 21.3g carbohydrates, <1g fiber, 7.6g sugar, 3g protein.

Sweet Potato Angel Biscuits

3   cups sweet potatoes (about 3 large)
      (cooked and mashed, keep
      warm)*
3   package active dry yeast
3/4 cup   warm water (105°F to 115°F)
7 1/2   cups all-purpose flour

1   Tbs. baking powder
1   Tbs. salt
1 1/2   cups sugar
1 1/2   cups shortening

Procedure

Combine yeast and warm water in a 2-cup liquid measuring cup; let stand 5 minutes. Sift flour and next 3 ingredients into a large bowl; cut in shortening with a pastry blender or fork until mixture is crumbly. Add yeast mixture and sweet potatoes, stirring until dry ingredients are moistened. Turn dough out onto a lightly floured surface; knead 5 minutes. Place dough in a lightly greased bowl, turning to grease top; cover and refrigerate 8 hours or overnight.

Roll dough to 1/2 inch thickness; cut with a 2-inch round cutter. Place on ungreased baking sheets; cover and let rise in a warm place (85°) free from drafts until doubled in bulk.

Preheat oven to 400° F. Bake for 10 to 12 minutes or until lightly browned.

Yield: 7 dozen

Nutrition Facts

Nutrition (per serving): 98 calories, 36 calories from fat, 4g total fat, 0mg cholesterol, 105.7mg sodium, 45.5mg potassium, 14.2g carbohydrates, <1g fiber, 4.1g sugar, 1.4g protein.

Tea Thyme Herb Scones

2	cups	all-purpose flour	1	tsp.	fresh rosemary, chopped
1/4	cup	fresh parsley -- chopped	1/4	tsp.	dried rosemary, crushed
1	Tbs.	granulated sugar	1/2	tsp.	salt
1	Tbs.	fresh thyme , chopped	1/3	cup	butter or margarine
1	tsp.	dried thyme	1/2	cup	milk
3	tsp.	baking powder	1		whole egg, slightly beaten

Procedure

Preheat oven to 400°. Lightly grease a cookie sheet.

In a large bowl, combine the flour, parsley, sugar, thyme, baking powder, rosemary and salt. Using a pastry blender or fork, cut in the margarine until the mixture resembles coarse crumbs. Stir in the milk and egg just until moistened.

On a floured surface, gently knead the dough 10 times. Place on the cookie sheet; roll or pat the dough into a 6-inch circle. Cut into 8 wedges; separate slightly.

Bake for 15 to 20 minutes, or until golden brown. Cut into wedges; serve warm.

Yield: 8 wedge scones

Nutrition Facts

Nutrition (per serving): 208 calories, 79 calories from fat, 9g total fat, 48mg cholesterol, 346.3mg sodium, 84.3mg potassium, 27.3g carbohydrates, 1.2g fiber, 2.5g sugar, 4.7g protein.

Treacle Scones

2 cups all-purpose flour

1/4 cup firmly packed dark brown sugar

1 1/2 tsp. baking powder

1/2 tsp. baking soda

1/4 tsp. ground cinnamon

1/4 tsp. ground nutmeg

1/4 tsp. salt

1/2 cup dried currants

1/4 cup unsalted butter

2 Tbs. treacle (dark molasses) (not blackstrap)

3/4 cup buttermilk

Topping

1/2 cup butter, melted

1/2 cup sugar

Procedure

Preheat oven to 400°F. Sift flour, dark brown sugar, baking powder, baking soda, cinnamon, nutmeg, and salt into a large bowl. Add dried currants. Melt 1/4 cup unsalted butter with dark molasses in heavy small saucepan over low heat. Combine molasses mixture with buttermilk and pour into dry ingredients. Mix dough until just blended.

Gently knead dough on generously floured surface until smooth. Divide dough into thirds. Pat out each dough piece into 4-inch diameter round. Cut each dough round into 4 wedges. Transfer dough wedges to ungreased cookie sheet, spacing 2 inches apart. Topping: Brush with melted butter. Sprinkle with sugar.

Bake at 400° for about 20 minutes or until firm to touch.

Yield: 12 wedge scones

Nutrition Facts

Nutrition (per serving): 261 calories, 104 calories from fat, 11.9g total fat, 31.1mg cholesterol, 236.9mg sodium, 167.7mg potassium, 36.6g carbohydrates, 1g fiber, 19.4g sugar, 3g protein.

Tropical Scones

1 1/2	cups	all-purpose flour	1/2 cup	toasted sunflower seeds (raw, unsalted)
1	tsp.	baking powder		
1/2 tsp.		baking soda	1/2 cup	white chocolate chips
1/8 tsp.		salt	1	whole egg, slightly beaten
3	Tbs.	butter, cold, cubed	1/2 cup	plain nonfat yogurt
3/4 cup		finely chopped mixed dried tropical fruit	1/4 tsp.	lemon zest, grated
			6 tsp.	sugar
1/4 cup		finely chopped dried pineapple		

Procedure

Preheat oven to 400°F. Spray cookie sheet with non-stick cooking spray. In large bowl, mix together flour, baking powder, baking soda and salt. Cut butter pieces into the flour until mixture resembles coarse meal. Stir in dried fruit, dried pineapple, sunflower seeds & chocolate chips. Set aside.

In medium sized bowl, whisk together egg, yogurt, lemon oil or zest and sugar. Add to flour-margarine mixture and mix just until moistened. Dough will be sticky. Flour hands slightly, shape into a round ball and flatten slightly. Place on prepared cookie sheet. With large serrated knife, cut into 8 pie pieces, but do not separate pieces. Bake 15-20 minutes or until golden and toothpick inserted into center comes out clean.

Yield: 8-12 scones

Nutrition Facts

Nutrition (per serving): 256 calories, 85 calories from fat, 10g total fat, 32.1mg cholesterol, 254.2mg sodium, 106.1mg potassium, 38.5g carbohydrates, 1.8g fiber, 12g sugar, 5.2g protein.

Victory Scones

2 cups all-purpose flour	1/4 cup applesauce
1/3 cup granulated sugar	2 Tbs. butter, melted
3 tsp. baking powder	1 tsp. almond extract
1/2 tsp. salt	1/2 cup almonds -- sliced
1 large egg	5 Tbs. strawberry or raspberry -- preserves
1/3 cup milk	Powdered sugar

Procedure

Preheat oven to 400°. Lightly grease a baking sheet.

Sift together the flour, sugar, baking powder and salt. Beat egg slightly in medium bowl and stir in milk, applesauce, margarine and almond extract. Stir applesauce mix and almonds into dry ingredients.

Drop dough by 1/4 cupsful about 3" apart onto cookie sheet. Pat into heart shapes about 3" wide and 1/2" high, using fingers dusted with flour. Make shallow well in center of each heart, using back of spoon dipped into flour. Place 1/2 teaspoon preserves in each well. Bake for 12-15 minutes or until golden brown. Dust with powdered sugar.

Yield: 12 heart-shaped scones

Nutrition Facts

Nutrition (per serving): 184 calories, 49 calories from fat, 5.7g total fat, 20.3mg cholesterol, 253.9mg sodium, 91.8mg potassium, 29.7g carbohydrates, 1.4g fiber, 6.3g sugar, 4.3g protein.

Yorktown Scones

2 cups all-purpose flour	1/2 cup finely chopped walnuts
1/4 cup firmly packed dark brown sugar	1/4 cup butter
1 1/2 tsp. baking powder	2 Tbs. dark molasses
1/2 tsp. baking soda	3/4 cup buttermilk
1/4 tsp. ground cinnamon	Melted butter
1/4 tsp. ground nutmeg	Sugar
1/4 tsp. salt	

Procedure

Preheat oven to 425°.

Sift flour, dark brown sugar, baking powder, baking soda, cinnamon, nutmeg, and salt into a large bowl. Add walnuts. Melt 1/4 cup unsalted butter with dark molasses in heavy small saucepan over low heat. Combine molasses mixture with buttermilk and pour into dry ingredients. Mix dough until just blended. Gently knead dough on generously floured surface until smooth.

Divide dough into thirds. Pat out each dough piece into a 4-inch diameter round. Cut each dough round into 4 wedges. Transfer dough wedges to ungreased cookie sheet, spacing 2 inches apart. Brush with melted butter. Sprinkle with sugar.

Bake until scones are just firm to the touch, about 20 minutes.

Yield: 12 wedge scones

Nutrition Facts

Nutrition (per serving): 247 calories, 130 calories from fat, 14.9g total fat, 31mg cholesterol, 236.2mg sodium, 141.3mg potassium, 25.4g carbohydrates, <1g fiber, 8.2g sugar, 4g protein.

Zesty Buttermilk Scones

3 cups all-purpose flour

1 Tbs. baking powder

½ cup sugar

1 tsp. salt

½ cup unsalted butter

1 cup prunes, finely chopped

1 zest of one lemon

2 whole eggs

GLAZE:

2/3 cup buttermilk

1 whole egg, beaten, plus 1 tsp. cream or milk to brush on scones

Procedure

Preheat oven to 375 degrees F. Sift all dry ingredients into a bowl. With your fingers or a pastry cutter, mix in the butter. Mix in the finely cut prunes and zest of one lemon. Shape a depression in the flour mixture, break in the eggs, and pour in the buttermilk. Using a spoon, slowly stir in the dry ingredients into the liquid in the middle until just blended. Do not over work. If the dough is too sticky, add additional flour.

Press the dough and form the scones in any form you wish (biscuit cutter or wedges). Brush the scones with egg and cream mixture. Bake for 18 to 20 minutes or until golden brown.

Yield: 28 scones

Nutrition Facts

Nutrition (per serving): 117 calories, 35 calories from fat, 4g total fat, 31.6mg cholesterol, 149.8mg sodium, 76.3mg potassium, 18.2g carbohydrates, <1g fiber, 6.3g sugar, 2.4g protein.

Recipe contributed by: Charles A. Caughlin

Welsh Cakes

4 cups all-purpose flour

1 1/2 cups sugar, plus 1 Tbs.

4 1/2 tsp. baking powder

1/2 tsp. salt

1/2 tsp. ground cinnamon

1/2 tsp. ground mace

1 cup butter, cold, finely diced

3/4 cup currants

1/2 cup mixed candied citrus peel, chopped

2 large eggs, slightly beaten

3/4 cup milk, approximately

Procedure

In a large bowl, sift together the flour, 1 ½ cups sugar, baking powder, salt, cinnamon, and mace. Add diced butter and blend until the mixture looks like coarse crumbs. Stir in the currants and mixed fruit peel. Add the beaten eggs and just enough milk to form a light dough.

On a lightly floured surface, knead the dough gently and roll to ¼-inch thickness. Using a 2 ½-inch cookie cutter, cut into rounds.

Preheat a lightly buttered griddle or electric frying pan to medium hot. Cook the Welsh Cakes for about 5 minutes per side or until they are golden brown, but still soft in the middle. Immediately after baking, sprinkle with reserved sugar.

Baking substitute: instead of stove stop, line a cookie sheet with parchment paper and bake Welsh Cakes for 8 to 10 minutes in a 350°F oven.

Yield: 40 Welsh Cakes

Nutrition Facts

Nutrition (per serving): 136 calories, 45 calories from fat, 5.5g total fat, 23mg cholesterol, 92mg sodium, 48mg potassium, 21g carbohydrates, >1g fiber, 12g sugar, 2g protein.

Bonus Recipe 1! Southern Biscuits

2 cups all-purpose flour	2 Tbs. unsalted butter, cold and diced small
4 tsp. baking powder	
1/4 tsp. baking soda	2 Tbs. shortening, cold and diced small
3/4 tsp. salt	
	1 cup buttermilk, chilled

Procedure

Preheat oven to 450° F.

In a large mixing bowl, combine flour, baking powder, baking soda and salt. Cut butter and shortening into dry ingredients until mixture resembles coarse crumbs. Make a well in the center and pour in the chilled buttermilk. Stir just until the dough comes together. The dough will be very sticky.

Turn dough onto floured surface, dust top with flour and gently fold dough over onto itself 5 or 6 times. Press into a 1-inch thick round. Cut out biscuits with a 2-inch cutter, being sure to push straight down through the dough. (Turning or twisting the cutter makes a deformed biscuit!) Place biscuits, barely touching, on a baking sheet. Reform dough scraps, working dough as little as possible and continue cutting.

Bake until biscuits are high and golden on top, 15 to 20 minutes.

Yield: 12 to 28 biscuits

Nutrition Facts

Nutrition (per serving): 81 calories, 27 calories from fat, 3g total fat, 4mg cholesterol, 238mg sodium, 36mg potassium, 12g carbohydrates, <1g fiber, <1g sugar, 1.9g protein.

Bonus Recipe 2! Blackberry Juice

2 quarts fresh blackberries
½ cup water

Procedure

In a 3-quart saucepan, bring blackberries and water to boil. Reduce heat and simmer for 5 minutes or until blackberries are soft.

Mash blackberries with a potato masher or fork; pour through a large wire mesh strainer lined with cheesecloth into a bowl, using the back of a spoon to squeeze out the juice. Discard the pulp and seeds.

Note: Substitute 2 (16-ounce) packages of frozen blackberries (thawed) when fresh blackberries are out of season.

Yield: 2 cups blackberry juice

Bonus Recipe 3! Marble Scones

4 cups all-purpose flour

1/3 cup sugar

4 tsp. baking powder

1 tsp. salt

1/2 tsp. baking soda

2/3 cup butter

1 1/3 cups buttermilk

2 tsp. vanilla extract

2 oz. semisweet chocolate, melted

Procedure

Preheat oven to 425 degrees F. Grease a baking sheet. In a large bowl, sift flour, sugar, baking powder, salt and baking soda. Cut in the butter until mixture resembles coarse crumbs. Remove 1/4 mixture to a bowl; reserve. Combine buttermilk and vanilla.

In a cup, combine 1/4 cup buttermilk mixture and melted chocolate. Add remaining buttermilk mixture to flour mixture in the large bowl and mix lightly with a fork until it forms soft dough. Add chocolate mixture to the reserved flour mixture in the medium bowl and stir with a fork until it forms soft dough. Turn both dough's onto a lightly floured surface.

Divide chocolate dough into 6 pieces. Dot 3 chocolate pieces over the plain dough. Fold plain dough over again and dot with the other 3 chocolate pieces; knead 6 times to marbleize dough.

Divide dough in half. With a floured rolling pin, roll each half into a 7-inch round; cut each round into 4 wedges. Place wedges one inch apart on prepared pan. Pierce tops with tines of a fork. Bake for 15 to 18 minutes or until golden brown. Serve warm.

Nutrition Facts

Nutrition (per serving): 450 calories, 11 calories from saturated fat, 19g total fat, 42mg cholesterol, 660mg sodium, 135mg potassium, 63g carbohydrates, 2g fiber, 11g sugar, 8g protein.

Cuppa Countess Guide for Tea

Blueberry Lemon Drop Scones

Cooking & Nutritional Tips

Common Kitchen Pans

When a recipe calls for...

4 cup baking dish:
- 9 inch pie plate
- 8 x 1¼″ layer cake pan
- 7⅜ x 3⅝ x 2¼″ loaf pan

6 cup baking dish:
- 8 or 9 x 1½″ layer-cake pan
- 10″ pie plate
- 8½ x 3⅝ x 2⅝″ loaf pan

8 cup baking dish:
- 8 x 8 x 2″ square pan
- 11 x 7 x 1½″ baking pan
- 9 x 5 x 3″ loaf pan

10 cup baking dish:
- 9 x 9 x 2″ square pan
- 11¾ x 7½ x 1¾″ baking pan
- 15 x 10 x 1″ jellyroll pan

12 cup baking dish or over:
- 12⅓ x 8½ x 2″ glass baking pan *(12 cups)*
- 13 x 9 x 2″ metal baking pan *(15 cups)*
- 14 x 10½ x 2½″ roasting pan *(19 cups)*

Total Volume of Various Special Baking Pans...

Tube Pans:
- 7½ x 3″ "Bundt" tube *(6 cups)*
- 9 x 3½″ fancy tube or "Bundt" pan *(9 cups)*
- 9 x 3½″ angel cake pan *(12 cups)*
- 10 x 3¾″ "Bundt" or "Crownburst" pan *(12 cups)*
- 9 x 3½″ fancy tube *(12 cups)*
- 10 x 4″ fancy tube mold (kugelhupf) *(16 cups)*
- 10 x 4″ angel cake pan *(18 cups)*

Spring Form Pans:
- 8 x 3″ pan *(12 cups)*
- 9 x 3″ pan *(16 cups)*

Ring Mold:
- 8½ x 2¼″ mold *(4½ cups)*
- 9¼ x 2¾″ mold *(8 cups)*

Charlotte Mold:
- 6 x 4¼″ mold *(7½ cups)*

Brioche Pan:
- 9½ x 3¼″ pan *(8 cups)*

Loaf Pan

Spring Form Pan

Layer-Cake Pan

Square Pan

Ring Mold

Brioche Pan

Charlotte Mold

Angel Cake Pan

Fancy Tube Mold (kugelhupf)

Bundt Pan

Equivalents for Cooking Ingredients

Apples (1 lb.)	3 or 4 medium
Bananas (1 lb.)	3 or 4 medium
Beans, dried (1 lb.)	5 to 6 cups cooked
Berries (1 quart)	3½ cups
Bread (1 slice)	½ cup crumbs
Cheese, grated (¼ lb.)	1 cup
Chocolate, 1 square (1 oz.)	1 T. melted
Cream (½ pint)	1 cup
Cream, heavy (1 cup)	2 cups whipped
Flour, all-purpose (1 lb.)	4 cups sifted
Gelatin (1 envelope)	1 T.
Herbs, dried (1 tsp.)	1 T. fresh
Lemon (2 to 3 T. juice)	1½ tsp. grated rind
Macaroni (1 cup dry)	2¼ cups cooked
Meat, diced (1 lb.)	2 cups
Mushrooms (1 lb.)	5 to 6 cups sliced
Nuts, shelled (¼ lb.)	1 cup chopped
Onion (1 medium)	½ cup chopped
Orange (6 to 8 T. juice)	⅓ to ½ cup pulp
Potatoes (3 medium)	1¾ to 2 cups mashed
Rice (1 cup uncooked)	3 cups cooked
Spaghetti (½ lb.)	3½ to 4 cups cooked
Sugar, confectioners (1 lb.)	4½ cups unsifted
Sugar, granulated (1 lb.)	2 cups
Tomatoes (1 lb.)	3 or 4 medium
Walnuts in shell (1 lb.)	1¾ cups chopped

Substitutions

For:	You Can Use:
1 T. cornstarch	2 T. flour *OR* 1½ T. quick cooking tapioca
1 C. cake flour	1 C. less 2 T. all-purpose flour
1 C. all-purpose flour	1 C. plus 2 T. cake flour
1 square chocolate	3 T. cocoa and 1 T. shortening
1 C. melted shortening	1 C. salad oil (may not be substituted for solid shortening)
1 C. milk	½ C. evaporated milk and ½ C. water
1 C. sour milk or buttermilk	1 T. lemon juice or vinegar and enough sweet milk to measure 1 C.
1 C. heavy cream	⅔ C. milk and ⅓ C. butter
1 C. heavy cream, whipped	⅔ C. well-chilled evaporated milk, whipped
Sweetened condensed milk	No substitution
1 egg	2 T. dried whole egg and 2 T. water
1 tsp. baking powder	¼ tsp. baking soda and 1 tsp. cream of tartar *OR* ¼ tsp. baking soda and ½ C. sour milk, buttermilk or molasses; reduce other liquid ½ C.
1 C. sugar	1 C. honey; reduce other liquid ¼ C.; reduce baking temperature 25°
1 C. miniature marshmallows	About 10 large marshmallows, cut up
1 medium onion (2½″ dia.)	2 T. instant minced onion *OR* 1 tsp. onion powder *OR* 2 tsp. onion salt; reduce salt 1 tsp.
1 garlic clove	⅛ tsp. garlic powder *OR* ¼ tsp. garlic salt; reduce salt ⅛ tsp.
1 T. fresh herbs	1 tsp. dried herbs *OR* ¼ tsp. powdered herbs *OR* ½ tsp. herb salt; reduce salt ¼ tsp.
Bread crumbs	Use crushed corn or wheat flakes, or other dry cereal. Or use potato flakes.
Butter	Use 7/8 cup of solid shortening plus 1/2 teaspoon of salt.

Substitutions

For:	You Can Use:
Fresh milk	To substitute 1 cup of fresh milk, use ½ cup each of evaporated milk and water. For 1 cup of whole milk, prepare 1 liquid cup of nonfat dry milk and 2½ teaspoons butter or margarine.
Sugar	Use brown sugar, although it will result in a slight molasses flavor.
Superfine sugar	Process regular granulated sugar in your blender.
Red and green sweet pepper	Use canned pimientos.
Vanilla extract	Use grated lemon or orange rind for flavoring instead. Or try a little cinnamon or nutmeg.
Flour	Substitute 1 tablespoon cornstarch for 2 tablespoons of flour. Or try using instant potatoes or cornmeal.
Buttermilk	Use 1 tablespoon of lemon juice or vinegar and enough fresh milk to make 1 cup. Let it stand 5 minutes before using.
Ketchup	Use a cup of tomato sauce added to 1¼ cups of brown sugar, 2 tablespoons of vinegar, ¼ teaspoon of cinnamon and a dash of ground cloves and allspice.
Unsweetened chocolate	Use 1 tablespoon of shortening plus 3 tablespoons of unsweetened chocolate to equal 1 square of unsweetened chocolate.
Corn syrup	Use ¼ cup of water or other type of liquid called for in the recipe, plus 1 cup of sugar.
Eggs	Add 3 or 4 extra tablespoons of liquid called for in the recipe. Or, when you're 1 egg shy for a recipe that calls for many, substitute 1 teaspoon of cornstarch.
Cake flour	Use ⅞ cup of all-purpose flour for each cup of cake flour called for in a recipe.
Fresh herbs and spices	Use ⅓ the amount of dried herbs or spices. Dried herbs are more concentrated.
Honey	To substitute 1 cup of honey, use 1¼ cups of sugar and ¼ cup of water or other liquid called for in the recipe.

Troubleshooting Baking Failures

Biscuits

1. Rough biscuits caused from insufficient mixing.
2. Dry biscuits caused from baking in too slow an oven and handling too much.
3. Uneven browning caused from cooking in dark surface pan (use a cookie sheet or shallow bright finish pan),too high a temperature and rolling the dough too thin.

Muffins

1. Coarse texture caused from insufficient stirring and cooking at too low a temperature.
2. Tunnels in muffins, peaks in center and soggy texture are caused from overmixing.
3. For a nice muffin,mix well but light and bake at correct temperature.

Cakes

1. Cracks and uneven surface may be caused by too much flour, too hot an oven and sometimes from cold oven start.
2. Cake is dry may be caused by too much flour, too little shortening, too much baking powder or cooking at too low a temperature.
3. A heavy cake means too much sugar has been used or baked too short a period.
4. A sticky crust is caused by too much sugar.
5. Coarse grained cake may be caused by too little mixing, too much fat, too much baking powder, using fat too soft, and baking at too low a temperature.
6. Cakes fall may be caused by using insufficient flour, under baking, too much sugar, too much fat or not enough baking powder.

7. Uneven browning may be caused from cooking cakes at too high a temperature, crowding the shelf (allow at least 2″ around pans) or using dark pans (use bright finish, smooth bottomed pans).
8. Cake has uneven color is caused from not mixing well. Mix thoroughly, but do not over mix.

Pies

1. Pastry crumbles caused by overmixing flour and fat.
2. Pastry is tough caused by using too much water and over mixing dough.
3. Pies can burn -for fruit or custard pies use a Pyrex pie pan or enamel pan and bake at 400° to 425° constant temperature.

Breads (Yeast)

1. Yeast bread is porous -this is caused by over-rising or cooking at too low a temperature.
2. Crust is dark and blisters -this is caused by over-rising, the bread will blister just under the crust.
3. Bread does not rise -this is caused from over-kneading or from using old yeast.
4. Bread is streaked -this is caused from underkneading and not kneading evenly.
5. Bread baked uneven -caused by using old dark pans, too much dough in pan, crowding the oven shelf or cooking at too high temperature.

Uses for Spices & Seasonings

All-Spice	Cakes, cookies, pies, breads, puddings, fruit preserves, pickles, relishes, yellow vegetables
Basil	Tomatoes, tomato sauce, barbecue sauce, salads
Celery Seed	Meat loaf; beef, lamb and vegetable stews; bean salad
Cloves	Ham, beets, pickling, beef marinades, hot spiced beverages, cakes, pies, puddings
Chili Powder	Vegetable and beef chili, cocktail and barbecue sauces, egg dishes, meatballs, meat loaf
Thyme	Chowder, seafood, stuffing, poultry, meat, vegetables
Dill	Salads and salad dressings, sour cream or mayonnaise dips, eggs, cucumbers, tomatoes, carrots, fish, cheese dishes
Garlic	Nearly all types of meat, fish, poultry, vegetables, sauces, stews, soups, salads and salad dressings
Rosemary	Lamb, poultry stuffing, beef and pork roasts, tomato sauce, salads, seafood, turnips, potatoes, cauliflower
Sage	Veal, sausage, poultry, stuffings, cheese spreads, soups
Tarragon	Salad dressings, sauces, egg dishes, stews, poultry, seafood
Cinnamon	Cakes, cookies, pies, puddings, coffee, dessert topping, yellow vegetables, hot spiced beverages

Food Storage

Baking Powder: Store the airtight tins in a cool, dry place and replace every 6 months.

Baking Soda: Store in an airtight container in a cool, dry place for about 6 months.

Beans: Once a package is opened, dry beans should not be refrigerated but stored in airtight containers in a cold, dry place. They will keep for about 1 year.

Bread: A rib of celery in your bread bag will keep the bread fresh for a longer time.

Brown Sugar: Wrap in a plastic bag and store in a tightly covered container for up to 4 months.

Cakes: Putting half an apple in the cake box will keep cake moist.

Celery and lettuce: Store in refrigerator in paper bags instead of plastic. Leave the outside leaves and stalks on until ready to use.

Cheese: Wrap cheese in a vinegar-dampened cloth to keep it from drying out.

Chocolate: Store chocolate for no longer than 1 year. It should be kept in a cool, dry place with a temperature range of 60°F to 75°F. If the storage temperature exceeds 75°F, some of the cocoa butter may separate and rise to the surface, causing a whitish color to the chocolate called "bloom".

Cocoa: Store cocoa in a glass jar in a dry and cool place.

Cookies: Place crushed tissue paper on the bottom of your cookie jar.

Cottage Cheese: Store carton upside-down. It will keep twice as long.

Dried Fruit: Store unopened packages of dried fruit in a cool, dry place or in the refrigerator. Store opened packages in an airtight container in the refrigerator or freezer for 6 to 8 months.

Flour: Store flour in a clean, tightly covered container for up to 1 year at room temperature.

Garlic: Garlic should be stored in a dry, airy place away from light. Garlic cloves can be kept in the freezer. When ready to use, peel and chop before thawing. Or, garlic cloves will never dry out if you store them in a bottle of cooking oil. After the garlic is used up, you can use the garlic flavored oil for salad dressing.

Granulated Sugar: Store sugar in a tightly covered container for up to 2 years.

Honey: Put honey in small plastic freezer containers to prevent sugaring. It also thaws out in a short time.

Ice Cream: Ice cream that has been opened and returned to the freezer sometimes forms a waxlike film on the top. To prevent this, after part of the ice cream has been removed press a piece of waxed paper against the surface and reseal the carton.

Lemons: Store whole lemons in a tightly sealed jar of water in the refrigerator. They will yield much more juice than when first purchased.

Limes: Store limes, wrapped in tissue paper, on lower shelf of the refrigerator.

Marshmallows: They will not dry out if stored in the freezer. Simply cut with scissors when ready to use.

Nuts: For optimum freshness and shelf life, nuts should be stored, preferably unshelled, in a tightly covered container in the refrigerator or freezer and shelled as needed. (The shell and the cool temperature keep the nut from turning rancid.)

Olive Oil: You can lengthen the life of olive oil by adding a cube of sugar to the bottle.

Food Storage

Onions: Wrap individually in foil to keep them from becoming soft or sprouting. Once an onion has been cut in half, rub the leftover side with butter and it will keep fresh longer.

Parsley: Keep fresh and crisp by storing in a wide-mouth jar with a tight lid. Parsley may also be frozen.

Popcorn: It should always be kept in the freezer. Not only will it stay fresh, but freezing helps eliminate "old-maids".

Potatoes: Potatoes, as well as other root vegetables, keep well in a dark, cool place, preferably a cellar. Store them in a dark brown paper bag.

Shredded Coconut: Store in a cool, dry place in an airtight container. Do not store in the refrigerator.

Smoked Meats: Wrap ham or bacon in a vinegar-soaked cloth, then in waxed paper to preserve freshness.

Soda Crackers: Wrap tightly and store in the refrigerator.

Strawberries: Keep in a colander in the refrigerator. Wash just before serving.

Vegetables with tops: Remove the tops on carrots, beets, etc. before storing.

Yeast: Store in the freezer or refrigerator in a closed plastic bag.

MEAT

Beef

Roasts	3 to 5 days
Steaks	3 to 5 days
Ground beef, stew meat	2 days

Pork

Roasts	3 to 5 days
Hams, picnics, whole	7 days
Bacon	7 to 14 days
Chops, spareribs	2 to 3 days
Pork sausage	1 to 2 days

Veal

Roasts	3 to 5 days
Chops	4 days

Lamb

Roasts	3 to 5 days
Chops	3 to 5 days
Ground lamb	2 days

Poultry

Chickens, whole	1 to 2 days
Chickens, cut up	2 days
Turkeys, whole	1 to 2 days

Cooked meats

Leftover cooked meats	4 days
Cooked poultry	2 days
Hams, picnics	7 days
Frankfurters	4 to 5 days
Sliced luncheon meats	3 days
Unsliced bologna	4 to 6 days

Measurements/Equivalents

Metric Volume Measurements

Measure	Equivalent
1 cubic centimeter	0.061 cubic inch
1 cubic inch	16.39 cubic centimeters
1 cubic decimeter	0.0353 cubic foot
1 cubic foot	28.317 cubic decimeters
1 cubic yard	0.7646 cubic meter
1 cubic meter	0.2759 cord
1 cord	3.625 steres
1 liter	0.908 qt. dry (1.0567 qts. liquid)
1 quart dry	1.101 liters
1 quart liquid	0.9463 liter
1 dekaliter	2.6417 gallons (1.135 pecks)
1 gallon	0.3785 dekaliter
1 peck	0.881 dekaliter
1 hektoliter	2.8378 bushels
1 bushel	0.3524 hektoliter

Simplified Measurements

1 tablespoon	3 teaspoons
2 tablespoons	1 ounce
1 jigger	1½ ounces
¼ cup	4 tablespoons
⅓ cup	5 tablespoons plus 1 teaspoon
½ cup	8 tablespoons
1 cup	16 tablespoons
1 pint	2 cups
1 quart	4 cups
1 gallon	4 quarts
1 liter	4 cups plus 3 tablespoons
1 ounce (dry)	2 tablespoons
1 pound	16 ounces

USDA Food Guide

Amounts in each food group are recommended for most adults at a daily 2,000 calorie level diet.

Food Group	USDA Daily Recommendation	Equivalent Amounts
Fruits	*2 cups (4 servings)*	**½ cup is equivalent to:** • ½ cup fresh, frozen or canned fruit • 1 medium fruit • ¼ cup dried fruit • ½ cup fruit juice
Vegetables	*2½ cups (5 servings)*	**½ cup is equivalent to:** • ½ cup raw or cooked vegetables • 1 cup raw leafy vegetables • ½ cup vegetable juice
Grains	*6 ounces*	**1 ounce is equivalent to:** • 1 slice bread • 1 cup dry cereal • ½ cup cooked rice, pasta or cereal
Meats & Beans	*5½ ounces*	**1 ounce is equivalent to:** • 1 ounce cooked lean meat, poultry or fish • 1 egg • ¼ cup cooked dry beans or tofu • 1 tablespoon peanut butter
Milk	*3 cups*	**1 cup is equivalent to:** • 1 cup low-fat or fat-free milk or yogurt • 1½ ounces low-fat or fat-free natural cheese • 2 ounces low-fat or fat-free processed cheese
Oils	*24 grams (6 teaspoons)*	**1 teaspoon is equivalent to:** • 1 teaspoon soft margarine • 1 tablespoon low-fat mayonnaise • 2 tablespoons light salad dressing • 1 teaspoon vegetable oil
Discretionary	*267 calories (2⅔ T. sugars)*	**1 tablespoon is equivalent to:** • 1 tablespoon jelly or jam • ½ ounce jelly beans • 8 ounces lemonade

The 2,000 calorie USDA Food Guide is appropriate for many sedentary males 51 to 70 years of age, sedentary females 19 to 30 years of age and for some other gender or age groups who are more physically active. The oils listed in this table are not considered to be part of discretionary calories because they are a major source of Vitamin E and polyunsaturated fatty acids, including the essential fatty acids, in the food pattern. In contrast, solid fats (i.e., saturated and trans fats) are listed separately as a source of discretionary calories.

Source: USDA Dietary Guidelines for Americans 2005, Table1.

Calorie Requirements Chart

Estimated amounts of calories required to maintain energy balance for certain gender and age groups at three different levels of physical activity. Estimates are rounded to the nearest 200 calories and were determined using the Institute of Medicine equation.

Gender	Age	Sedentary	Activity Level Moderately Active	Active
Child	2 to 3	1,000	1,000 to 1,400	1,000 to 1,400
Female	4 to 8	1,200	1,400 to 1,600	1,400 to 1,800
	9 to 13	1,600	1,600 to 2,000	1,800 to 2,200
	14 to 18	1,800	2,000	2,400
	19 to 30	2,000	2,000 to 2,200	2,400
	31 to 50	1,800	2,000	2,200
	51+	1,600	1,800	2,000 to 2,200
Male	4 to 8	1,400	1,400 to 1,600	1,600 to 2,000
	9 to 13	1,800	1,800 to 2,200	2,000 to 2,600
	14 to 18	2,200	2,400 to 2,800	2,800 to 3,200
	19 to 30	2,400	2,600 to 2,800	3,000
	31 to 50	2,200	2,400 to 2,600	2,800 to 3,000
	51+	2,000	2,200 to 2,400	2,400 to 2,800

Source: *USDA Dietary Guidelines for Americans 2005, Table 3.*

How Much is One Serving?

Milk & Milk Products
- 1 C. (8 oz.) milk or yogurt
- 2 (¾ oz.) slices cheese (⅛″ thick)
- 2 C. cottage cheese
- 1½ C. ice cream or frozen yogurt

Meat & Meat Alternatives
- 2 to 3 oz. cooked lean meat, poultry or fish
- 2 eggs
- 7 oz. tofu
- 1 C. cooked dried beans or peas
- 4 T. peanut butter
- ½ C. nuts or seeds

Vegetables
- ½ C. cooked vegetables
- ½ C. raw chopped vegetables
- 1 C. raw leafy vegetables
- ½ to ¾ C. vegetable juice

Fruits
- 1 whole medium fruit (about 1 cup)
- ¼ C. dried fruit
- ½ C. canned fruit
- ½ to ¾ C. fruit juice

Bread & Cereal
- 1 slice bread
- 1 medium muffin
- ½ hot dog bun or hamburger bun
- ½ bagel or English muffin
- 4 small crackers
- 1 tortilla
- 1 C. cold cereal
- ½ C. cooked cereal
- ½ C. rice
- ½ C. pasta

Source: *USDA Dietary Guidelines for Americans 2005, Table 3.*

Table of Nutrients

Estimated nutrient intake levels recommended by the USDA at the daily 2,000 calorie level, as well as recommendations by the Institute of Medicine (IOM) for females 19 to 30 years of age.

Nutrient	USDA	IOM for females 19 to 30*
Protein, g	91	RDA: 56
Carbohydrate, g	271	RDA: 130
Total Fat, g	65	–
Saturated Fat, g	17	–
Monounsaturated Fat, g	24	–
Polyunsaturated Fat, g	20	–
Total Dietary Fiber, g	31	AI: 28
Cholesterol, mg	230	ALAP
Potassium, mg	4,044	AI: 4,700
Sodium, mg	1,779	AI: 1,500, UL:<2,300
Calcium, mg	1,316	AI: 1,000
Magnesium, mg	380	RDA: 310
Iron, mg	18	RDA: 18
Phosphorous, mg	1,740	RDA: 700
Zinc, mg	14	RDA: 8
Riboflavin, mg	2.8	RDA: 1.1
Vitamin B6, mg	2.4	RDA: 1.3
Vitamin B12	8.3	RDA: 2.4
Vitamin C	155	RDA: 75
Vitamin E	9.5	RDA: 15
Vitamin A	1,052	RDA: 700

*RDA= Recommended Daily Allowance, AI= Adequate Intake, AMDR= Acceptable Macronutrient Distribution Range,
UL= Upper Limit, ALAP= As Low As Possible while consuming a nutritionally adequate diet.

Source: USDA Dietary Guidelines for Americans 2005, Table 2.

Sources for Common Nutrients

Vitamin A
- Bright orange vegetables like carrots, sweet potatoes and pumpkin
- Tomatoes, tomato products and red sweet peppers
- Leafy greens, such as spinach, collards, turnip greens, kale, beet and mustard greens, green leaf lettuce and romaine
- Orange fruits like mango, cantaloupe, apricots and red or pink grapefruit

Vitamin C
- Citrus fruits and juices, kiwi fruit, strawberries, guava, papaya and cantaloupe
- Broccoli, peppers, tomatoes, cabbage (especially Chinese cabbage), brussels sprouts and potatoes
- Leafy greens, such as romaine, turnip greens and spinach

Potassium
- Baked white or sweet potatoes, cooked greens or spinach, orange squash
- Bananas, plantains, many diced fruits, oranges and orange juice, cantaloupe and honeydew melons
- Cooked dry beans
- Soybeans (green and mature)
- Tomato products (sauce, paste or puree)
- Beet greens

Source: USDA Dietary Guidelines for Americans 2005, Table 5.

Healthy Choices

This table shows the differences in saturated fat and calorie content of commonly consumed foods. Comparisons are made between foods in the same food group.

Food Group	Portion	Saturated Fat (g)	Calories
CHEESE Regular Cheddar cheese	1 oz.	6.0	114
Low-fat Cheddar cheese	1 oz.	1.2	49
MEATS & POULTRY Regular ground beef	3 oz.	6.1	236
Extra lean ground beef	3 oz.	2.6	148
Fried chicken leg	3 oz.	3.3	212
Roasted chicken breast	3 oz.	0.9	140
Fried fish	3 oz.	2.8	195
Baked fish	3 oz.	1.5	129
MILK Whole milk	1 C.	4.6	146
Low-fat milk (1%)	1 C.	1.5	102
BREADS Croissant	Medium	6.6	231
Oat bran bagel (4″)	Medium	0.2	227
DESSERTS Regular ice cream	½ C.	4.9	145
Low-fat frozen yogurt	½ C.	2.0	110
OILS Butter	1 tsp.	2.4	34
Soft margarine	1 tsp.	0.7	25

Source: *USDA Dietary Guidelines for Americans 2005, Table 9.*

Sources of Saturated Fat

This table shows major dietary sources of saturated fats in the U.S. diet, with a mean average daily intake of 25.5 grams. Saturated fats make the body produce more cholesterol, which can raise blood cholesterol levels and lead to cardiovascular disease. Contribution shows percent of total saturated fat consumed.

Food Group	Contribution	Food Group	Contribution
Cheese	13.1	Shortening	4.4
Beef	11.7	Salad Dressing/Mayonnaise	3.7
Milk	7.8	Poultry	3.6
Oils	4.9	Margarine	3.2
Ice Cream/Sherbet /Frozen Yogurt	4.7	Sausage	3.1
Cakes/Cookies /Quick Bread /Donuts	4.7	Potato Chips/Corn Chips/Popcorn	2.9
Butter	4.6	Yeast Bread	2.6
		Eggs	2.3

Source: *USDA Dietary Guidelines for Americans 2005, Table 10.*

Physical Activity Recommendations

Physical Activity Recommendations Per Age Group

Children & Adolescents
Engage in at least 1 hour of physical activity on most or all days of the week.

Pregnant Women
In the absence of medical or obstetric complications, engage in 30 minutes or more of moderate-intensity physical activity on most or all days of the week. Avoid activities with a high risk of falling or abdominal trauma.

Breastfeeding Women
Be aware that neither acute nor regular exercise will adversely affect the mother's ability to successfully breastfeed.

Older Adults
Engage in regular physical activity to reduce functional declines associated with aging.

Source: *USDA Dietary Guidelines for Americans 2005, Physical Activity, viii.*

Engaging in regular physical activity will promote your health, psychological well-being and a healthy body weight. Use the following recommendations for achieving regular physical activity.

- To reduce the risk of chronic disease in adulthood, engage in at least 30 minutes of moderate-intensity physical activity. Physical activity should be above usual activity at work or home on most days of the week.

- Greater health benefits can be achieved by most people by engaging in more vigorous physical activity over a longer duration.

- To help manage body weight and to prevent gradual unhealthy weight gain in adulthood, engage in approximately 60 minutes of moderate to vigorous intensity activity on most days of the week, while not exceeding caloric intake requirements.

- To sustain weight loss in adulthood, participate in at least 60 to 90 minutes of daily moderate-intensity physical activity while not exceeding caloric intake requirements.

- Achieve physical fitness by including cardiovascular conditioning, stretching exercises for flexibility and resistance exercises or calisthenics for muscle strength and endurance.

Calories Expended in Common Physical Activities

This table shows the average amount of calories expended during common physical activities. Examples are average amounts of calories a 154-pound individual will expend by engaging in each activity for 1 hour. The expenditure value encompasses both resting metabolic rate calories and activity expenditure. Some of the activities can constitute either moderate- or vigorous-intensity physical activity depending on the rate at which they are carried out (for example, walking or biking).

Moderate Physical Activity	Approximate Calories Expended Per Hour
Hiking	370
Light gardening/yard work	330
Dancing	330
Golf (walking while carrying clubs)	330
Bicycling (<10 mph)	290
Walking (3.5 mph)	280
Weight lifting (general light workout)	220
Stretching	180

Vigorous Physical Activity	
Running/jogging (5 mph)	590
Bicycling (>10 mph)	590
Swimming (slow freestyle laps)	510
Aerobics	480
Walking (4.5 mph)	460
Heavy yard work (chopping wood)	440
Weight lifting (vigorous effort)	440
Basketball (vigorous)	440

Source: *USDA Dietary Guidelines for Americans 2005, Table 4.*

With Teacup and Books in Hand..

Andrew F. Smith, E. (2004). *Oxford Encyclopedia of Food and Drink in America* (Vol. 2). New York: Oxford University Press.

Dameron, J. D. (2003). *King's Mountain.* Cambridge, Massachusetts: Da Capo Press.

Fitzgerald, K. S. (2004). *America's Founding Food: The Story of New England Cooking.* Chapel Hill: University of North Carolina Press.

John Frederick Schroeder, D. (1854). *Maxims of Washington.* New York, New York: Sprinkle Publications.

Johnson, D. (2002). *Tea & Etiquette* (Revised Edition 2002 ed.). Herndon, Virginia: Capital Books, Inc.

L.Williamson, M. (1995). *Life and Anecdotes of George Washington.* Harrisonburg, Virginia: Sprinkle Publications.

Messick, H. (1976). *King's Mountain* (First ed.). Yadkinville, North Carolina: Little, Brown & Company.

Pettigrew, J. (2001). *A Social History of Tea.* London: The National Trust Enterprises.

Pratt, J. N. (1999). *New Tea Lover's Treasury.* San Francisco, California, USA: Publishing Technology Associates.

Ramsey, R. W. (1964). *Carolina Cradle.* Charlotte, North Carolina, U.S.A.: The University of North Carolina Press.

Ray, W. S. (1950). *Tennessee Cousins.* Austin, Texas: Genealogical Publishing Co., Inc.

Tony Mack McClure, P. (1999). *Cherokee Proud.* Somerville, Tennessee, USA: Chunannee Books.

Recipe Notes

Gift Order Form

Order additional copies of this cookbook as an ideal gift for family and friends.

Send check or money order along with Gift Order Form below to:

17-76 Tea Party Award-Winning Recipes
c/o Tea Trade Mart
800 NE Tenney Rd 110-107
Vancouver, WA 98685
360-433-9454
Or order online at http://www.teatrademart.com
(Phone number and e-mail is required for shipping confirmation.)

- →

Please send me _____ copies of your cookbook
At $19.95 each or 3 Cookbooks at $14.95 each
Plus $3 shipping and handling per book ordered.
Mail books to:

Name or Business Name: _____

Address: _____

City: _____ State _____ Zip _____

Your Phone Number: _____

E-mail Confirmation: _____

- _____ I am interested in selling your books in my store. Please contact me.